Cavaliers and Roundheads

Three hundred years ago, Britain was torn by violent civil war, as king and parliament struggled for power.

In this book, the author tells how heated arguments in parliament lead to open warfare. Father fights against son, brother against brother. Cromwell's "plain russet-coated captains," with their close-cropped hair and stern demeanour, face the fiery charges of plumed Cavaliers. The great battles of Edgehill, Marston Moor and Naseby move back and forth, with pikemen and musketeers fighting in the mud. Despite a few sweeping successes, the Cavaliers are slowly crushed by the iron discipline of the New Model Army. King Charles is captured, tried, and executed. A Commonwealth is set up. Yet still the fighting goes on, as army and parliament battle for supremacy, and Cavaliers in exile await their chance to return.

In fact, peace was not restored to the war-torn realm till nearly twenty years after the troubles began, when another Charles Stuart was crowned King, and parliamentary government was renewed.

A WAYLAND SENTINEL BOOK

Cavaliers and Roundheads

Michael Gibson

"I go from a corruptible to an incorruptible
crown, where no disturbance can be."
*Words spoken by Charles I just before his execution
(30th January, 1649)*

WAYLAND PUBLISHERS LONDON

More Sentinel Books

The Story of Gunpowder *Kenneth Allen*
The Legions of Rome *Matthew Holden*
Tourney and Joust *Steven Jeffreys*
Nelson's Navy *Roger Hart*
A Medieval Siege *Steven Jeffreys*
War in the Trenches *Matthew Holden*
Genghis Khan and the Mongols *Michael Gibson*
The Wars of the Roses *Kenneth Allen*
The Battle of Britain *Anthony Hobbs*
The Crusades *Matthew Holden*
Battle of the Atlantic *Kenneth Allen*
The French Foreign Legion *Nigel Thomas*
The Samurai of Japan *Michael Gibson*
The Desert Rats *Matthew Holden*
The Story of the Navy *Anthony Hobbs*

frontispiece: Charles I leaving Westminster Hall after receiving notice of his execution (1649).

SBN 85340 198 5

Copyright © 1973 by Wayland (Publishers) Ltd.
101 Grays Inn Road London WC1
Set in 'Monophoto' Baskerville and
printed offset litho in Great Britain by
Page Bros (Norwich) Ltd, Norwich

Contents

List of Illustrations

Introduction

The Anabaptift The Brownift

The Familift   The Papift

Above A seventeenth-century cartoon shows the Bible being tossed up and down in a blanket by the different religious sects. Religion was a great cause of disagreement during this period, and played an important part in the Civil War.
Opposite The arrest of Guy Fawkes, who was going to blow up the Houses of Parliament in protest against the religious policies of James I (1605).

Throughout the Middle Ages, the kings of England ruled with the help of only a few powerful nobles. Gradually, however, parliament acquired more power. All taxes and new bills had to be approved by both the House of Lords and the Commons, and signed by the king before they became law. By Tudor times, the members of parliament were growing discontented – they were mostly well-educated and experienced in the ways of the world, and wanted a real share in the government of their country.

Kings were free to appoint and dismiss their ministers as they chose. The countryside was controlled by Lords Lieutenant and Justices of the Peace, but these important local government officers were both untrained and unpaid. There was no permanent army or police force, and kings had to rely on the cooperation of their subjects to maintain peace.

However, during the sixteenth century, several developments caused increasing friction between the Crown and the English people. Between 1480 and 1640, there was a steep rise in prices. The upper classes were particularly hard hit because they lived on fixed incomes. Although they owned vast estates, the rents from them rose much more slowly than prices.

Even more disturbing were the religious disagreements known as the Reformation. Until the reign of Henry VIII (1509–47), the English had been Roman Catholic, and owed allegiance to the Pope in Rome. But King Henry made himself head of the English Church instead of the Pope, and many Englishmen became Protestants. When Queen Elizabeth came to the throne in 1558, she tried to reconcile the Catholics and Protestants by setting up the Anglican Church, but this only made matters worse. The Catholics, Anglicans and Puritans (or extreme Protestants) remained stubbornly hostile to each other.

King James I (1603–25) inherited a very difficult situation. Prices continued to rise. Angry Catholics tried to blow up the Houses of Parliament. Unhappy Puritans emigrated to America. Discontented members of parliament refused to vote the King any taxes until he had granted their requests. James was too old and tired to cope with these difficulties. The English people looked forward to his death, hoping that the new King would be a more effective ruler.

1. King versus parliament

Unfortunately, the new King, Charles I (1625–49), lacked all the qualities of a strong ruler. He had been brought up in the shadow of his brilliant elder brother Henry, who had died unexpectedly of typhoid in 1612. Charles walked with a slight limp and spoke with a bad stammer. He was not very intelligent, and couldn't see that England was changing. He believed that he was God's representative on earth, and that anyone who dared to disagree with him was automatically in the wrong.

Above Charles I's favourite, the Duke of Buckingham, walks through Portsmouth just before his assassination. The Duke was very unpopular, and was stabbed by an out-of-work officer. Can you see the dagger poised above his left shoulder?

His only real friend was the handsome Duke of Buckingham. Charles was dazzled by his friend's charm and elegance, and made him his chief minister. This was a grave mistake. Before he knew it, Buckingham had involved England in a war with Spain and France. Defeat followed humiliating defeat, and the people murmured angrily. The King, however, couldn't bear criticism of his beloved favourite. In 1628, the Duke was stabbed to death by an out-of-work officer. When the King heard the news he was heart-broken but, while he wept, the common people celebrated the death of the man they had hated. Charles never forgave them.

The King was desperate for money. He had quarrelled with his first parliament when it only offered him the right to collect customs duties on wine and wool, known as tonnage and poundage, for a year, instead of for life as had been customary previously. His second parliament proved just as difficult so he dismissed that too, and started to collect money illegally. When some gentlemen refused to lend him the money he demanded, he clapped them into prison. This caused such widespread discontent that the members of his third parliament drew up the Petition of Right, in which they pointed out that no man should be asked to pay a tax that hadn't been approved by parliament. Charles was forced to sign this document before parliament would vote him the subsidies he urgently needed.

When the Commons went on to attack other aspects of royal policy, Charles ordered the Speaker to adjourn. But several burly members grabbed the Speaker and held him in his chair until the House had finished its debate. Charles was so deeply angered by this act of defiance that he refused to call another parliament for eleven years.

Above Charles I, who came to the throne in 1625, was not strong enough nor intelligent enough to deal with all the problems his country was facing.

Right This contemporary cartoon shows Archbishop Laud dining off Prynne's ears. Prynne was a Puritan whose ears were cut off when he dared to criticize the government's religious policy.

The eleven years' tyranny

Charles now had to find new ways of raising money. According to medieval law, gentlemen whose revenue exceeded £40 a year were obliged to become knights, and Charles started to fine all those who had failed to apply for this honour. He also discovered through studying old maps that many landowners had encroached on the royal forests, and they too were fined.

More valuable still was Ship Money, an emergency tax levied on people living in seaports, the proceeds of which Charles spent on building a splendid new fleet. Many people were convinced that the King had broken the law in order to raise this money for himself, and a man called John Hampden challenged the legality of the tax. His case was heard by twelve of the country's chief judges. In spite of considerable royal pressure, the judges only supported the King by seven votes to five. As a result, more and more people refused to pay Ship Money.

Taxation was only one cause of popular discontent. Religion was another. The Archbishop of Canterbury, William Laud, a fussy little man, tried to make everybody worship God in the same way. The Archbishop's men visited churches throughout the land, forcing the priests to use the Anglican prayer book. As a result several thousand Puritans emigrated

Below left The great ship *Sovereign of the Seas*, one of the many fine vessels built by Charles I with the Ship Money he collected from seaports around the country.

to America in order to escape persecution, and those that remained became gradually more embittered. Three Puritans called Prynne, Bastwicke and Burton were savagely whipped and had their ears cut off for daring to criticize the government's religious policy.

While Laud tried to discipline the English, his colleague, Thomas Wentworth, was sent to Ireland. Wentworth was a masterful man and soon reduced the Irish to obedience. But, in the process, he created many enemies, both for himself and for the King.

If Wentworth's policy in Ireland was ill-advised, Charles's in Scotland was disastrous. The King ordered the Scots to use a new prayer book similar to the English one. The Scots refused. Charles decided to punish them, and ordered his Lords Lieutenant to raise the county militia. Although a large army was soon collected, it lacked training and the will to fight. The King was defeated and obliged to make peace.

This short Bishops' War exhausted the King's treasury, so that he was forced to recall parliament to obtain more money. The Eleven Years' Tyranny was over.

Breakdown

Parliament, when it met, was in no easy mood. Its members were not prepared to grant the King any taxes until their grievances had been dealt with. Charles soon lost patience and again dissolved parliament.

By this time, a group of highly intelligent men led by John Pym had gathered to oppose the King. They got into touch with the Scots who marched south and defeated Charles at the battle of Newburn. The Scots insisted that the King should pay for the upkeep of their army while a treaty was being negotiated. As Charles couldn't do this without parliament's help, he was forced to call his fifth and last parliament. The opposition leaders set to work to destroy his dictatorial powers. Thomas Wentworth was arrested and accused of treason. All forms of unparliamentary taxation were abolished. The royal courts of the Star Chamber and the High Commission were closed down. Finally, an act was passed so that parliament could neither be adjourned nor dissolved without its own consent.

So far the members of parliament had been united. When they came to deal with religious questions, however, divisions soon appeared in their ranks. The Puritans wanted to see the Anglican Church radically changed, while the Anglicans were equally determined that it should remain exactly as it was.

Gradually, a group of moderates led by Sir Edward Hyde formed around the King. These men felt that parliament had gone far enough, and that any further changes would upset the balance of the constitution. Charles himself still hoped to regain all of his lost powers, but his many plots to do so had destroyed parliament's trust in him.

Pym and his supporters then decided that it was time to force Charles into the open, and show the

Below Charles I marches into the House of Commons to arrest the five members who had accused the Queen of high treason. But, as the King remarked bitterly, "The birds are flown."

world what kind of man he was. Accordingly, they accused the Queen, Henrietta Maria, of high treason. As they had expected, Charles was beside himself with fury and stormed down to the House of Commons to arrest the five members responsible. On entering the Chamber, Charles looked round and remarked bitterly, "The birds are flown." Pym and his followers had already escaped.

Charles left the capital in disgust and marched north. Now there was nothing for it but to prepare for war.

Conflicting loyalties

Throughout 1642, men all over England had to decide whom to support, the King or parliament. The Royalists, supporters of the King, became known as Cavaliers, because many of them were mounted on fine horses. The Parliamentarians, on the other hand, were called Roundheads, because they often wore their hair short and close-cut to the head, in contrast to the long-flowing locks of the Cavaliers.

Some men followed the King out of a sense of

Below This contemporary cartoon shows a confrontation between Prince Rupert's dog "Pudel" and the Roundhead dog "Peper." But loyalties were not always so clear-cut during the Civil War, and many people changed sides several times.

loyalty. Sir Edmund Verney, for example, said: "I have eaten his bread and served him near thirty years and will not do so base a thing as to forsake him." Others like Oliver Cromwell gave their support to parliament. Even Cromwell, though, had to admit that he wasn't sure what he really wanted: "I can tell you, sir, what I would not have, though I cannot what I would."

Father fought against son, brother against brother, friend against friend. Sir William Waller, a Roundhead, wrote to Sir Ralph Hopton, a Cavalier: "My affections for you are so unchangeable that hostility itself cannot violate my friendship, but I must be true to the cause which I serve."

Some people were so confused by the complexity of the situation that they changed sides several times. However, these heart-searchings were usually confined to the upper classes. As Sir Arthur Haselrigg commented acidly: "They [the ordinary people] care not what government they live under, so long as they may plough and go to market." Their attitude, however, soon changed. Although the English Civil War lacked many of the horrors of modern warfare, few areas escaped from it unscathed. The soldiers on both sides went about looting, raping and ravaging. In many country areas, the ordinary people were so incensed that they joined the gangs of clubmen, who used to ambush unwary soldiers and thrash them.

On the other hand, the Civil War opened up new opportunities. It was soon found that courage and military skill were not the monopoly of the aristocracy. Oliver Cromwell vowed: "I had rather have a plain russet-coated captain that knows what he fights for and loves what he knows, than that which is called a gentleman and is nothing else."

2. Preparations for war

On leaving London, Charles made his way north to Hull, where he hoped to arm his men with weapons from the city's arsenal. However, the governor resolutely refused to open the city gates, and the disappointed King was forced to march on to Nottingham, where he had ordered all men who could bear arms to meet him. When he arrived there on 22nd August, there were scarcely any volunteers waiting for him. Undaunted, he raised the Royal Standard, but this proud symbol of monarchy was blown down during the night. The people murmured that this was a warning. No good would come of the war.

While the King strode about the midlands trying to raise an army, his Queen toured the courts of Europe. She hoped to persuade the Kings of France and Spain to provide her husband with money and troops to put down his rebellious subjects. They, for their part, were prepared to give her sympathy but little else. Moreover, the magnificent fleet Charles had built policed the seas around Britain with such efficiency that few Royalists managed to penetrate its defences.

On land, both sides were arming themselves. Parliament appointed the experienced Earl of Essex as commander-in-chief of their forces. He had fought in Holland and Germany, and knew well how to handle professional troops. But his hurriedly-assembled regiments were an untrained rabble, who didn't know one end of a pike from another. Moreover, there wasn't just one Parliamentarian army but several. The Fairfaxes raised one in Yorkshire,

Above Charles I orders the Royal Standard to be erected on the ramparts of Nottingham Castle (22nd August, 1642).

the Earl of Manchester another in East Anglia, and Sir William Waller a third in the West Country.

Affairs were just as chaotic on the Royalist side. Lord Ruthven, the commander-in-chief, was an old man. Without doubt the most important of the Cavalier generals was Prince Rupert of the Rhine, King Charles's nephew. Although he was still only twenty-two in 1642, Prince Rupert had been fighting as a soldier since he was thirteen. He was a ruthless, arrogant and dashing commander, who inspired his men to great deeds. In the short time available to them, the rival commanders worked hard to turn their raw recruits into trained soldiers.

19

Pikemen

Pikemen formed the backbone of most seventeenth-century armies. Their pikes were formidable weapons, sixteen feet long with long wooden shafts and sharp steel points. The pikemen wore helmets, breast and back plates, neck armour and thigh pieces. In hand-to-hand fighting where their pikes were useless, they defended themselves with cheap swords. Since they were expected to march in full armour for long distances, they had to be exceptionally tall and strong.

At the beginning of a battle, the pikemen took up position in the centre of the army, and formed into squares. While the rival cavalry forces charged at each other, the pikemen advanced in formation towards the enemy ranks and tried to decide the battle by "push of pike." Soon, both sides were so inextricably mixed up that friend struggled with friend in the vicious hand-to-hand fighting.

Often, while they were thus locked in battle, the cavalry thundered down to attack their exposed flanks. It was then that their hours of drill were put to the test. The men at the end of the line turned half round and presented their pikes to the new danger. They needed all possible courage as the wall of horses came charging towards them. All they could do was to push the butts of their pikes firmly into the ground, grip the shafts till their knuckles shone white with the strain, and wait for the sickening shock of impact.

Sometimes, the horsemen paused to fire their pistols into the packed ranks of infantry before drawing their swords and charging. If the pikemen remained calm and resolute, the cavalry would impale themselves on the glittering steel points. The air was filled with the screams of the wounded and the ground covered with the dead and dying. As the battle ebbed and flowed, the pikemen trampled backwards and forwards, crushing beneath their feet the bodies of friend and foe alike.

And so the murderous affair continued until one side or the other drew off or they were forced apart by the darkness of evening. For the dead, there was a hurried burial in an unremembered grave, for the wounded little chance of recovery, and for the living the prospect of just such another bloodbath not far in the future.

Opposite An officer of English pikemen, in full regimental dress.
Below A pikeman in a typical position, as he waits for the cavalry to charge down on him. Provided he doesn't give way, the horses will impale themselves on the sharp steel point of his pike.

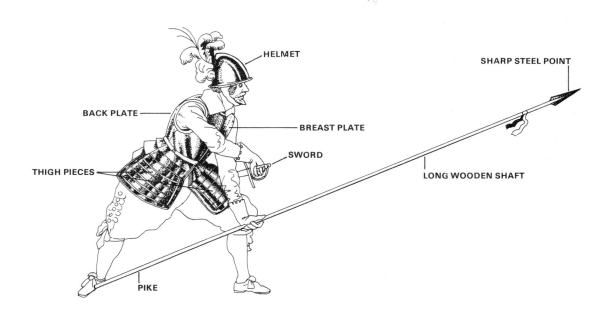

HELMET

SHARP STEEL POINT

BACK PLATE

BREAST PLATE

SWORD

THIGH PIECES

LONG WOODEN SHAFT

PIKE

Musketeers

At the time of the Civil War, musketeers had only recently been introduced. They wore little armour, and expected the pikemen to protect them during enemy cavalry charges. At close quarters, they would draw their swords, or beat down their opponents with the butts of their muskets.

At the beginning of the Civil War, most musketeers used matchlock guns which were loaded at the muzzle. A charge of powder and a lead ball or bullet were rammed down the barrel with a ramrod, and wedged in place by a plug. The gun was primed by pouring a little highly inflammable powder into the touchhole. When the trigger was pulled, a curved metal arm holding a lighted cord (or match) came into contact with the priming. The powder ignited, the flame flashed along the channel into the barrel, and the charge was detonated and expelled the bullet.

Although muskets were heavy, unwieldy weapons, they were carried resting on the left shoulder like a modern rifle. The musketeer had to support the barrel on a wooden rest to aim his weapon. It took a long time to load, aim and fire, and the musketeers were usually arranged in several ranks. The front line fired while the others were loading. Then it stepped aside so that the next rank could come forward and fire. Very careful training was needed to make this routine efficient.

The musketeers had to be able to service their weapons. Whenever possible, they made their own bullets by heating up some lead and pouring it into the moulds they carried around with them. Their charges of gunpowder had to be carefully measured since overcharged muskets were likely to explode, killing everybody within reach. The charges were

Guard, blow and open your pan.   *Present.*   *Give Fire.*

Above This illustration from a seventeenth-century manual of arms drill shows three of the stages followed by musketeers when priming and firing their weapons.
Below A musketeer prepares to fire his matchlock.

wrapped in screws of paper and fitted into a broad belt or bandolier which the musketeers slung across their shoulder. The powder horns containing the priming had special grooves, "cut-outs," which only allowed enough powder for one loading to pass out of the nozzle at a time. The matches were made out of cord, which was dipped into spirits and sulphur to make it burn slowly and steadily.

The musketeers were specialists. Their numbers steadily increased during the Civil War until they daunted cavalry and infantry alike by their murderous fire.

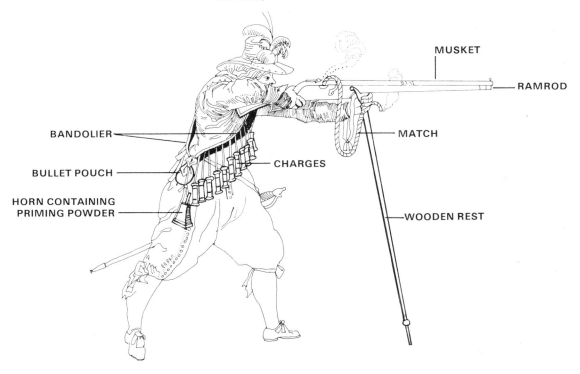

BANDOLIER

BULLET POUCH

HORN CONTAINING
PRIMING POWDER

CHARGES

MUSKET

RAMROD

MATCH

WOODEN REST

The cavalry

The cavalry were the élite of the army. They were well-armed, well-equipped and well-mounted. They wore back and breast plates, strong neck defences, thigh pieces and gauntlets. Even so, they were still not completely protected from the swords, pikes and muskets of their enemies. Beneath their armour, they wore tough leather coats to stop their bodies from being rubbed raw by the metal plates.

The heavily armoured cavalrymen, known as cuirassiers, were dying out even before the Civil War, since it was increasingly difficult to find horses strong enough to carry them. Moreover, if they were unhorsed in battle, they had the greatest difficulty in remounting.

Every trooper or cavalryman carried a pair of heavy pistols, which could fire one shot apiece. The lance was no longer popular and was only used by Scottish cavalry – the English made do with good-quality swords. In addition, many men carried with them small battleaxes which could cut through thick armour.

The cavalry were used as shock troops. The Roundheads usually trotted up to the enemy and discharged their pistols before charging. The Cavaliers, on the other hand, tended to put their trust in cold steel and charged at a full gallop. There was something to be said for both tactics. The Roundheads did considerable damage with their pistol volley and were able to control their final charge. However, the Cavaliers' thunderbolt charge had much greater penetration even though it did mean the horsemen were virtually impossible to control.

The cavalry was the pride of the army, and

Above The cavalry were the élite of the army, and were used mainly as shock troops. Here, Cromwell leads his troopers in a charge at the battle of Marston Moor (1644).

attracted many dashing gentlemen to its ranks, but its task was formidable. Horsemen were sent in to attack the squares of infantry, and had to face the murderous fire of the musketeers. When they reached the hedge of pikes, many more met their deaths skewered on the cruel points. Others were dragged from their saddles and butchered – each pike bore a hook especially for this purpose.

B

The dragoons

As well as cavalry, every army also had a division of mounted infantrymen, the dragoons. They were mounted on poor quality horses commonly known as nags, and were armed with cheap swords and carbines. Like the musketeers, they wore little or no armour.

They took their name from their carbines, which were originally called "dragons." These had shorter barrels and wider bores than ordinary muskets. However, their main advantage lay in their flint-locks which replaced the lighted match of earlier muskets with a hammer containing special flints. When the trigger was pulled, the hammer snapped down onto a metal plate and threw up a shower of sparks. These fell on the gunpowder in the pan and ignited it, and this fired the bullet. The flintlock was far more reliable than the old matchlock, and could even be fired from the saddle.

When the army was on the march, the dragoons rode ahead of the main body, scouring the country-side for food and fodder. This meant that they often

26

clashed with local civilians, and soon had earned themselves an evil reputation for looting, burning and raping. They were supposed to capture and occupy all the key points along the route, such as bridges and passes, until the rest of the army arrived. In camp, they guarded the most exposed positions since they were able to escape on horseback and give the warning when they saw superior enemy forces approaching.

Before a battle, the dragoons searched the neighbouring woods, copses and hedgerows for enemy musketeers. In this way, they frequently saved their comrades from being caught in an enfilade – murderous fire directed from the flank of a force and raking it from end to end. Such attacks could destroy whole units in a few minutes.

In an emergency, dragoons could even act as cavalry, and often played a crucial part in battles by suddenly charging an unsuspecting enemy. During a retreat, they usually formed the rearguard. They dismounted and covered their comrades' withdrawal, keeping the enemy at bay by their steady, accurate fire. The dragoons were some of the most hard-working and useful soldiers in the army.

Opposite Dragoons were some of the most hard-working units in the army. Here a group of them fire over the heads of their horses to accustom them to battle conditions (from *Military Instructions* by N. Burt, 1644).

Below The firing mechanism of a flintlock musket. When the trigger was pulled, the hammer containing the flints would hit against the metal plate, and cause a shower of sparks. These would then fall onto the gunpowder in the flash-pan, and ignite it.

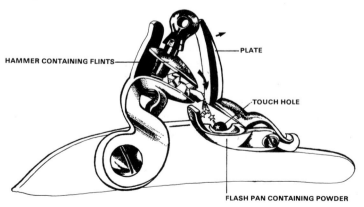

HAMMER CONTAINING FLINTS

PLATE

TOUCH HOLE

FLASH PAN CONTAINING POWDER

The artillery

There were four or five main types of cannon used during the Civil War. The heaviest of these was the culverin. This could fire a ball weighing between sixteen and twenty pounds some 2,000 yards. However, the culverin was difficult to load, and could only be fired ten or twelve times an hour. The demi-culverins were more popular than their bigger brothers. They fired a ball some ten pounds in weight, and were most effective at ranges of up to 350 yards. More common still were the light field-guns, the sakers, minions and drakes, which fired balls weighing six, three and two pounds respectively.

All these cannon were mounted on heavy wooden carriages, and were extremely difficult to move. In wet weather, they sank into the mud and often rolled over. Going uphill, they tore at their ropes, and even broke through them. Rolling down slopes, they threatened to run away and crush everything in front of them. Because of these difficulties, they often failed to reach the main body of the army in time to play any part in the battle.

Gun crews consisted of three men: the gunner, his mate and a helper. They charged their weapons with ready-made cartridges or loose powder. Range finding was very difficult. Each cannon used to throw slightly to the left or to the right, and the

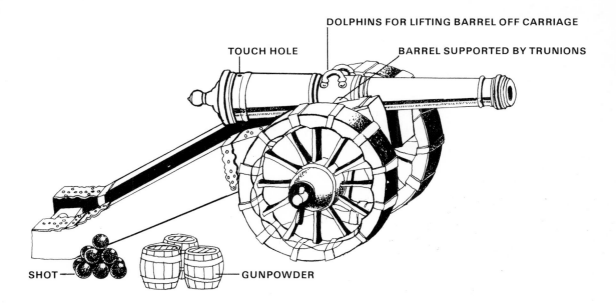

DOLPHINS FOR LIFTING BARREL OFF CARRIAGE

TOUCH HOLE

BARREL SUPPORTED BY TRUNIONS

SHOT

GUNPOWDER

Above A cannon mounted on its wooden carriage. During the Civil War, cannon were not considered very reliable – they were difficult to move, and dangerous to fire.

Opposite Firing a cannon, from a seventeenth-century woodcut. Many small details could affect a gun's accuracy – the shape and size of the ball, the heat of the barrel, and so on – and the gunner had to take all these into account when firing.

gunner had to get to know his weapon really well so that he could take these characteristics into account when firing.

The crew had to watch out for the recoil when the gun jumped back after firing. Sometimes cannon were even hurled over backwards. They had also to be careful to sponge out all the burning fragments in the barrel before reloading, otherwise the cartridge or powder would explode in their faces.

In battle, the cannon were usually placed in the spaces between the cavalry and the infantry. It was the gunners' job to break up the enemy formations, although in this they rarely succeeded. In fact, after the preliminary bombardment, the gunners were relatively useless since their view was blocked by their own troops. In these circumstances, they were particularly exposed to attack, and victorious armies frequently captured their opponents' artillery.

The day of the cannon was still to come.

3. Civil war

For some days in October, 1642, the Roundhead
and Cavalier armies marched side by side without
either knowing it. Then the Royalists caught a
glimpse of the Roundheads through a gap in the
hills. Shortly afterwards, the Earl of Essex saw the
Cavaliers deploying along the slopes of Edgehill.

The Roundhead general drew up his men in the
meadows before the village of Kineton, with his
cavalry on either side of his infantry brigades. His
flanks were protected by thickets containing Roundhead musketeers and dragoons. The whole force

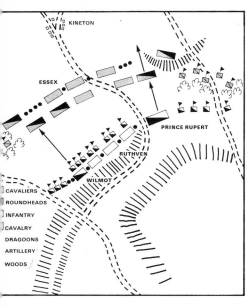

Above Plan of the battle of
Edgehill (1642).

Left Prince Rupert leads the
Cavaliers in a charge against
the left wing of the Roundhead
cavalry at the battle of
Edgehill. Unfortunately, the
Prince couldn't keep control of
his men, and they went on to
loot the enemy baggage train
instead of returning to the
fight.

wore orange scarves to distinguish them from the
Cavaliers.

Lord Ruthven, the Royalist commander, formed
his army into a single line. He massed his infantry
in the centre and placed his cavalry on either wing,
with a screen of dragoons beyond them. His cannon
were sited in the spaces between the infantry com-
panies.

Sir Jacob Astley, a Royalist, prayed: "O Lord,
thou knowest how busy I must be this day. If I
forget thee, do not thou forget me." At two o'clock,
the battle opened with a cannonade. Then Prince
Rupert attacked and destroyed the left wing of the
Roundhead cavalry. Unfortunately, the Prince
couldn't then stop his undisciplined men from looting
the enemy's baggage train. Meanwhile, the other
Cavalier cavalry under Wilmot charged and scattered the Roundheads' right wing. In despair,
Essex seized a pike and marched forth, grimly
determined to die on the battlefield.

All, however, was not lost. In their haste, the
Cavaliers hadn't noticed Essex's reserve cavalry,
who suddenly attacked the Royalist infantry with
such ferocity that the royal standard bearer, Sir
Edmund Verney, was killed. Even in death, he
continued to grip the flagstaff like a vice, so that the
jubilant Roundheads had to cut off his hand in
order to bear away their trophy.

Now it was the turn of the Cavaliers to feel
despair. But just then the Royalist cavalry straggled
back onto the field. Their attacks saved the brave
Cavalier infantry from annihilation. Nightfall parted
the two exhausted armies. Victory had fallen to
neither side.

Turnham Green

The next morning, the Earl of Essex decided not to renew battle with the Cavaliers. As far as he was concerned, London was the key to the situation and he saw it as his duty to protect the capital from attack. So the Roundheads stole away while it was still dark, and left the Cavaliers in possession of the battlefield. The Royalists were too badly mauled, however, to follow him, and instead made their way to Oxford where Charles then set up his head-quarters.

Prince Rupert still hoped to capture London. His flying columns of cavalry moved up and down the Thames Valley spreading fear wherever they went. But by the time the Royalists finally made their effort it was too late. They found themselves facing the trained bands of London, some 24,000 men, in an entrenched position to the west of the city, at Turnham Green. The odds against a Royalist victory were too great, and the King retired to Oxford for the winter.

Elsewhere things went better for the King. Sir Ralph Hopton drove the Roundheads out of Corn-wall and entered Devon, where he threatened the Roundhead stronghold of Plymouth. The Earl of Newcastle crossed the River Tees and entered York-shire. The Earl was a man of immense wealth and power, but he was no soldier. The road to London was open but, instead of seizing this valuable opportunity, he spent his time trying to corner the Yorkshire Roundheads.

During the winter, Charles and his generals drew up a plan of campaign for the coming year. Sir Ralph Hopton was to move through the southern counties to Kent, the Earl of Newcastle was to march

Above During the Civil War, Charles I set up his headquarters at Oxford, a Royalist stronghold. This picture shows him in conference at Oxford with one of his supporters, Edward Hyde, 1st Earl of Clarendon, who later wrote a history of the war.

south to Essex, while the King himself was to attack and destroy the main Roundhead army before driving east. All three armies were then to join together near London, and launch a combined assault on the capital. Charles was convinced that, if London fell, the war would be brought to an end. However, before any of this could come to pass, the Roundhead centres of Plymouth, Hull and Bristol had first to be captured. None of the Cavalier generals were prepared to leave their own lands a prey to an enemy behind their lines.

33

The Ironsides

When Lord Grey of Groby took command of the Eastern Association of counties loyal to parliament (Norfolk, Suffolk, Essex, Hertford and Cambridge), he promoted Oliver Cromwell to the rank of colonel, and asked him to raise two troops of cavalry.

Cromwell chose his officers and men with great care. His captains had to be "godly honest men," and his troopers "men of spirit." By ancient law all able-bodied men of sixteen or over were liable for military service. Both the King and parliament preferred to enrol volunteers but, as there were never enough of these available, many men were

Above Oliver Cromwell, the most famous of the Roundhead leaders, in a portrait by Robert Walker.

34

pressed into service. Local landlords persuaded their tenants to join the colours by threats and even by brute force. Cromwell, however, would not use such crude recruiting methods. His men had to join him of their own free will, because they believed in the justice of his cause.

His standards were high. A contemporary newssheet noted: "No man swears but he pays twelve pence; if he be drunk, he is set in the stocks or worse; if one calls the other Roundhead he is cashiered." But Cromwell's harshness was fully justified – troopers had a terrible reputation. Contemporaries complained about their "firing of towns, ravishing of women, stealing and violent taking."

Loyalty was essential. Cromwell made this clear right from the start by having a couple of deserters publicly whipped in the town square at Huntingdon. However, he also took a fatherly interest in his troops. In 1643, he warned the mayor of Colchester that "the foot and dragooners are ready for mutiny" for lack of pay and provisions. These were duly provided.

Cromwell's men were equipped with helmets, and back and breast plates. Their only weapons were swords and pistols. He considered himself an excellent judge of horseflesh, and bought all the cavalry horses himself. He also made sure that they were properly looked after – his troopers had to feed and groom their mounts before they were allowed to eat and rest themselves.

The Ironsides were the finest soldiers in the Roundhead army.

A soldier's life

The pay of an ordinary soldier was appalling. In 1644, Roundhead infantrymen were paid no more than eightpence a day (the equivalent of 4p.), dragoons one shilling and sixpence ($7\frac{1}{2}$p.), and cavalrymen two shillings (10p.). This wasn't even enough to pay for their food and lodging. Officers were slightly better off. A colonel received a pound a day, a lieutenant-colonel fifteen shillings (75p.), a major thirteen shillings (65p.), a captain eight shillings (40p.), and a lieutenant four shillings (20p.). No wonder there was so much looting – it was the only way most soldiers could make enough money to live on.

Soldiers on the march rarely had tents. If they were near a town, they were billeted on the protesting citizens. In the country, they had to bivouac wherever they could. A Roundhead wrote in 1643: "I thank my God I find as much comfort and health lying under a hedge and suffering hunger, thirst and cold as when I lay on a feather bed and fared well."

At the beginning of the Civil War, the only regiments with uniforms were those raised by wealthy gentlemen at their own expense. Uniforms

Left Life for the common soldier in the seventeenth century was very hard. The pay was low, the conditions of work appalling. And, if he dared to complain, as the soldiers in this picture are doing, the punishments were harsh and brutal.

cost about two pounds each – a lot of money in those days – which was deducted from the soldier's pay at a rate of tuppence (1p.) a day.

Discipline was harsh. Whipping was the usual punishment. A court martial could award anything up to sixty lashes for a minor offence. Sometimes offenders had to run the gauntlet. This meant that they were forced to race between two files of soldiers who hit them with cudgels as they went past. Mutiny and insubordination carried the death penalty.

Neither side had a medical corps so the surgeons, if there were any, were civilians. There were no anaesthetics, and the wounded had to be forcibly held down while the surgeons went about their grisly work. If they had time, the patients used to fill themselves up beforehand with drink to dull the pain. Nothing at all was known about germs. The surgical instruments were usually unclean, and many soldiers died from infected wounds.

There was little help either for the disabled. Each parish was supposed to look after its own veterans. But, for most of them, this meant nothing more than a licence to beg.

The three-pronged attack

In the west of the country, great progress was made by the Cavaliers. Sir Ralph Hopton overran Devon and came face to face with his old friend and enemy, Sir William Waller, at Roundway Down on 13th July. The Roundheads were defeated and left the Cavaliers in control of all of the west except Plymouth.

Meanwhile, Prince Rupert captured Bristol after a four-day siege. Only the city of Gloucester now stood between the King and London. As soon as the Earl of Essex heard of Gloucester's plight, he marched across the Cotswolds, and relieved the city. Then both armies raced for London.

The Roundheads found the Cavaliers barring their way through the Berkshire Downs south-east of Newbury, and here, on 20th September, 1643, the second great battle of the Civil War was fought. The Royal musketeers stationed themselves in the tangled woods and lanes. From these natural defences, they poured a deadly hail of fire onto the unfortunate Roundheads as they dragged themselves through the mud to attack their positions. Then the Royalists ran short of ammunition, and the Roundheads pushed them back up the slopes. For a time, it looked as if the Cavaliers would be beaten. But Rupert arrived in the nick of time and drove the Roundhead cavalry from the field. However, when he turned on the Roundhead infantry, it was a very different story. He charged again and again without success – the soldiers had taken refuge in the same hedges and lanes that had previously served his own infantry so well. The sweating troops stumbled backwards and forwards over the same ground all day. At nightfall, the Cavaliers retreated to the safety of Newbury.

Next morning, Essex set out towards London. After three miles, Rupert fell upon the rearguard. In the ensuing panic, the Roundhead cavalry rode into their own foot-soldiers. But, once again, the Roundhead musketeers saved the day, and repulsed the Cavaliers with heavy losses. Essex was able to continue his march unhindered.

So the second part of the royal plan was only partially successful. Everything depended on the success or failure of the Earl of Newcastle and his Whitecoats on their march south from Yorkshire.

Below Prince Rupert gives encouragement to his troops at the storming of Bristol, which only fell after a difficult four-day siege (1643).

A Solemn LEAGUE AND COVENANT,

for Reformation and defence of Religion, the Honour and happinesse of the king and the Peace and safety of the three kingdoms of ENGLAND, SCOTLAND and IRELAND.

We Noblemen, Barons, Knights, Gentlemen, Citizens, Burgesses, Ministers of the Gospel and Commons of all sorts in the kingdoms of England, Scotland and Ireland, by the Providence of God living under one King and being of one reformed Religion, having before our eyes the Glory of God and the advancement of the kingdome of our Lord and Saviour Iesus Chryst, the Honour and happinesse of the Kings Majesty and his posterity, and the true publique Liberty, Safety and Peace of the kingdoms wherein every ones private Condition is included, and calling to minde the treacherous and bloody Plots, Conspiracies, Attempts, and Practices of the Enemies of God against the true Religion and professors thereof in all places, especially in these three kingdoms ever since the Reformation of Religion, and how much their rage, power and presumption are of late, and at this time increased and exercised, whereof the deplorable estate of the Church and kingdome of Ireland, the distressed estate of the Church and Kingdom of England, and the dangerous estate of the Church and Kingdom of Scotland, are present and publique Testimonies; We have now at last, after other means of Supplication, Remonstrance, Protestations and Sufferings, for the preservation of our selves and our Religion from utter Ruine and Destruction, according to the commendable practice of these Kingdoms in former times and the Example of Gods people in other Nations; After mature deliberation, resolved and determined to enter into a mutuall and solemn League and Covenant, Wherein we all subscribe and each one of us for himselfe with our hands lifted up to the most high God, do sweare.

I. That we shall sincerely, really and constantly, through the Grace of God endeavour in our severall places and callings the preservation of the Reformed Religion in the Church of Scotland, in Doctrine, Worship, Discipline & Government, against our common Enemies; the reformation of Religion in the kingdoms of England and Ireland in Doctrine, Worship, Discipline and Government, according to the Word of God, and the Example of the best Reformed Churches; And shall endeavour to bring the Churches of God in the three kingdoms to the neerest conjunction and Uniformity in Religion, Confession of Faith, Form of Church-government, Directory for Worship and Catechising, That we and our posterity after us may as Brethren live in Faith and Love and the Lord may delight to dwell in the midst of us.

II. That we shall in like manner without respect of persons indeavour the extirpation of Popery, Prelacie that is Church government by Arch Bishops, Bishops their Chancellors and Comissaries, Deans, Deans and Chapters, Archdeacons & all other Ecclesiasticall Officers depending on that Hierarchy, Superstition, Heresie, Schisme, Prophanenesse and whatsoever shall be found to be contrary to sound Doctrine and the power of Godlinesse lest we partake in other mens sins and therby be in danger to receive of their plagues, and that the Lord may be one and his Name one in the three kingdoms.

III. We shall with the same sincerity, reality and constancy in our severall Vocations, endeavour with our estates and lives mutually to preserve the Rights and Priviledges of the Parliaments and the Liberties of the kingdoms, and to preserve and defend the kings Majesties person and authority in the preservation and defence of the true Religion, and Liberties of the kingdoms that the World may beare witnesse with our consciences of our Loyaltie, and that we have no thoughts or intentions to diminish his Majesties just power and greatnesse.

IV. We shall also with all faithfulnesse endeavour the discovery of all such as have beene, or shall be Incendiaries, Malignants, or evill Instruments by hindering the Reformation of Religion, dividing the king from his people, or one of the kingdoms from another, or making any faction or parties amongst the people contrary to this league & Covenant that they may be brought to publick triall and receive condigne punishment as the degree of their offences shall require or deserve, or the supreame Iudicatories of both kingdoms respectively or others having power from them for that effect, shall judge convenient.

V. And whereas the happinesse of a blessed Peace between these kingdoms denyed in our times to our Progenitors is by the good Providence of God granted unto us and hath been lately concluded and setled by both Parliaments we shall each one of us according to our place and interest, indeavour that they may remain conioyned in a firm Peace or an Union to all posterity. And that Iustice may be done upon the wilfull Oppossers thereof in manner expressed in the precedent Article.

A threefold cord is not easily broken

England
Scotland
Ireland

VI. We shall also according to our places & callings in this common cause of Religion, Liberty and Peace of the kingdomes, assist and defend all those that enter into this League and Covenant in the maintaining & pursuing thereof and shall not suffer our selves directly or indirectly by whatsoever combination, perswasion or terror to be devided & withdrawn from this blessed Union & conjunction, whether to make defection to the contrary part or to give our selves to a detestable indifferency or neutrality in this cause which so much concerneth the glory of God, the good of the kingdoms and honour of the king, but shall all the dayes of our lives zealously and constantly continue therein against all oppossition, and promote the same according to our power against all Lets and impediments whatsoever, and what we are not able our selves to suppresse or overcome we shall reveale and make known that it may be timely prevented or removed. All which we shall doe as in the sight of God.

And because these kingdoms are guilty of many sins & provocations against God & his Son Iesus Christ, as is too manifest by our present distresses and dangers the fruits thereof We professe and declare before God and the world our unfained desire to be humbled for our & for the sins of these kingdoms especially that we have not as we ought valued the inestimable benefit of the Gospel, that we have not laboured for the purity and power thereof and that we have not endeavored to receive Christ in our hearts nor to walk worthy of him in our lives which are the causes of other sins and transgressions so much abounding amongst us. And our true and unfained purpose desire and endeavour for our selves and all others under our power and charge both in publick and in private in all duties we owe to God and man to amend our lives and each one to goe before another in the Example of a reall Reformation that the Lord may turne away his wrath and heavy indignation and establish these Churches and kingdoms in truth and peace. And this Covenant we make in the presence of almighty God the Searcher of all hearts with a true intention to performe the same as we shall answer at that great day when the secrets of all hearts shall be disclosed. Most humbly beseeching the Lord to strengthen us by his holy Spirit for this end and to blesse our desires and proceedings with such successe as may be deliverance and safety to his people and encouragement to other Christian Churches groaning under or in danger of the yoake of Antichristian tyranny to joyne in the same or like Association and Covenant to the glory of God the enlargement of the kingdom of Iesus Chryst and the peace and tranquility of Christian Kingdoms & Commonwealths.

THE SOLEMN LEAGUE AND COVENANT, ILLUSTRATED BY W. HOLLAR, 1643.

The struggle in the east

In fact, the Earl made but slow headway in face of determined resistance by the forces raised in Yorkshire by the Fairfax family. This gave Oliver Cromwell the opportunity he needed to prove himself.

On 13th May, 1643, he met a small force of Cavaliers near Grantham. "Since they were not advancing towards us," he wrote, "we agreed to charge them." The Royalists broke and fled after a brief but bitter struggle. This was Cromwell's first victory. Then a Cavalier army laid siege to Gainsborough in Lincolnshire. Cromwell was sent to the city's aid. On sighting the enemy, he charged immediately without even giving his men time to form into battle order. "At last," he wrote, "they a little shrinking our men, perceiving it, pressed in upon them and immediately routed the whole body."

While the Earl of Newcastle was held up by stern resistance outside Hull, Cromwell and Sir Thomas Fairfax joined forces to attack the Cavaliers near Winceby. Cromwell, who led the first line of cavalry, had his horse shot under him. As he picked himself up, he was knocked down a second time by a Royalist trooper. While he was still desperately searching for a new mount, Fairfax charged the enemy in the flank. In half an hour it was all over. Curiously enough, it was Cromwell and not Fairfax who was given the credit for this victory.

But all this was of little importance compared with John Pym's last triumph. Although the great politician was by now dying of cancer, he concluded an alliance with the Scots, the Solemn League and Covenant, by which the Scots agreed to provide a large army in support of the Parliamentarians on condition that the English Church was reformed.

The tide had turned against the King.

Opposite An illustrated version by W. Hollar of the "Solemn League and Covenant for reformation and defence of religion, the honour and happiness of the King, and the peace and safety of the three kingdoms of England, Scotland and Ireland" (1643). By this agreement, the Scots promised to support parliament against the King, and this represented a great blow to Royalist hopes of success.

Rupert's ride

At the beginning of 1644, all attention was focussed on the north of England where the Scots and the Roundheads were closing in on the Earl of Newcastle. The Earl, fearing that he would be trapped in York, appealed to Rupert for help.

Rupert's ride through Lancashire was one long triumph. While he plundered Stockport and stormed Bolton and Liverpool, the Roundhead generals waited for him in Yorkshire. There were three armies in front of York – the Scots under Lord Leven, the Eastern Association under the Earl of Manchester, and the northern army under Fairfax.

When Rupert reached Knaresborough, the Roundheads threw their forces across the road to York. Rupert, however, rode north to Boroughbridge, crossed the River Ouse there, and entered York unopposed. His opponents were deeply shocked. It was one of the most brilliant manoeuvres of the whole war.

Rupert wanted to attack the Roundheads before they could recover their confidence, so he asked the Earl of Newcastle to be ready to march with him against the enemy at four o'clock the next morning. This was a bad mistake. Newcastle was a proud man, and took umbrage at this perfunctory treatment. Consequently, he made no effort to move his famous Whitecoats at the right time.

The Earl finally joined Rupert at 9 o'clock the next morning, but without his infantry. Rupert was all for attacking the Roundheads there and then while they were still in a state of confusion, but when Newcastle objected, the Prince gave way. This was his second mistake.

Dauentry

Brimidgham

Right This contemporary woodcut shows Prince Rupert on his way from Daventry to Birmingham. There was much looting and plundering by soldiers during the Civil War, and most people did not welcome the army coming their way.

During the long day, the Royalist infantry slowly made its way from York to Marston Moor, which gave the Roundheads time to reorganize themselves. Nevertheless, by half past four, all the Cavaliers were in position so Rupert called for an immediate attack. Once again, he allowed himself to be overruled by his cautious colleagues.

By half past seven, silence had fallen upon both armies and it seemed certain that there would be no battle that day. Rupert allowed his men to break ranks and prepare their evening meal, while he retired to his quarters at the rear. This was his fourth and fatal mistake.

Marston Moor

As the sun went down, Cromwell charged at the head of 2,000 men of the Eastern Association. They thundered down on the Royalists' right wing and scattered its first line like dust. When Rupert found his men retreating, he shouted: "Swounds, do you flee? Follow me!", and led the second line into battle.

For a moment, it seemed as if Rupert would defeat the Roundheads. Cromwell, blinded by a gun flash and wounded in the neck, had had to retire to the rear. But, at the crucial moment, 800 Scots under David Leslie charged the Cavaliers. This gave the Roundheads time to face about and renew their attack. For a few minutes, the two sides remained locked in battle, swords flailing. At last the Royalists broke, and the Prince only just escaped.

On the other side of the field, the story was very different. The Cavaliers led by Goring, a hard-drinking swashbuckler, smashed Sir Thomas Fairfax's cavalry and set about looting the baggage train. In the centre, the two great blocks of infantry struggled in a sea of mud. The senior Roundhead generals then decided that all was lost and fled.

By this time, however, Cromwell had recovered, and he made his way round to Goring's old position.

44

Here, he found Sir Thomas Fairfax, covered in blood from a sword-cut across the face. The two men led the cavalry in a furious charge upon the rear of Goring's surprised troopers. The Cavaliers fled.

Newcastle's brave Whitecoats were surrounded, but fought on until 10 o'clock at night when the last of them was cut down. When the defeated Cavalier generals met in the darkness, they asked Rupert: "What will you do?" "I'll rally my men," replied the Prince. By morning, he had collected together some 7,000 cavalry whom he led south.

Cromwell boasted to his brother-in-law: "We never charged but we routed the enemy. God made them as stubble to our swords." The result was a disaster for the royal cause. The north was lost. It was the most decisive battle of the war and confirmed Cromwell's reputation.

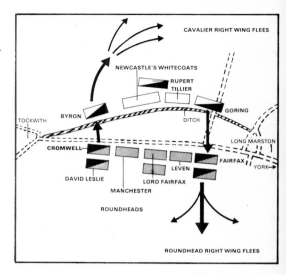

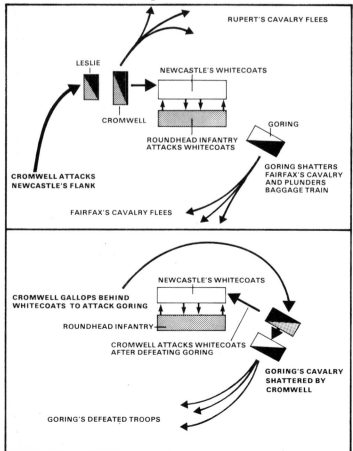

Above and left The three main stages of the battle of Marston Moor (1644) – a disaster for the Royalist cause.

Opposite The standard was always an important rallying point during a battle. Here, fierce fighting is taking place around the royal standard at Marston Moor.

An opportunity lost

The Roundhead leaders made no attempt to follow up their great victory, and the Cavaliers managed to stage a comeback in the south. The Earl of Essex marched to Devonshire to raise the siege of Plymouth, and then made the mistake of invading Royalist Cornwall. As a result, he was trapped in Fowey. On 31st August, his cavalry managed to escape thanks to the negligence of the drunken Goring. Essex deserted his command and sailed to London, but Philip Skippon, his infantry commander, was forced to surrender on 2nd September.

As a result, the King was able to return to the Thames Valley and save the beleaguered Royalist strongholds there. Meanwhile, the Roundheads at last united their forces, and Waller, Manchester and Essex decided to attack and destroy the King's army before Rupert could join him. The Cavaliers had only 10,000 men to the Roundheads' 19,000.

Charles drew up his army before Newbury with considerable skill. In order to reach him the Round-heads had to fight their way through a maze of narrow country lanes under heavy fire from the royal musketeers and the cannon of Donnington Castle. Manchester was so slow in sending reinforcements that the Roundhead attack failed.

Next day, Manchester could have dealt the King a crushing blow. But when he learned that the royal army was drawing off towards Oxford, he only yawned and said that it was too late to do anything about it. Cromwell raged to his brother-in-law: "We have some amongst us much slow in action; if we could [attend to] our own ends less, and our ease too, our business in this army would go [much faster]."

46

In November, Cromwell savagely attacked the generals' blunders in parliament. As a result, it was decided that no member of the House of Lords or the Commons should hold any military command as long as the war lasted. This decision became known as the Self-Denying Ordinance. In fact, Parliament made exceptions to its terms and many men including Cromwell retained their commands. The time, however, had clearly come to reorganize the army.

Right A contemporary portrait of Philip Skippon, one of the most able of the Roundhead commanders, who later rose to great prominence during the Commonwealth period.

Opposite This engraving of Cromwell was based on a portrait by Van Dyke showing Charles I on horseback. Cromwell was a great judge of horseflesh, and always liked to choose his troops' horses himself.

The new New Model Army

During the spring of 1645, the Roundheads set about creating the New Model Army. Sir Thomas Fairfax was appointed its commander-in-chief, with Cromwell as Lieutenant-General of Horse, and Philip Skippon as Sergeant-Major General of Foot. A proper intelligence system was set up under Scoutmaster General Watson. Just as important as the fighting services was the administration or commissariat. The Commissary for Provisions kept the army supplied with food and drink, while the Carriage-Master-General organized the baggage train. All the other officers' ranks were decided by their length of service, and the inefficient were ruthlessly rejected.

There were eleven cavalry regiments, each 600-men strong, and a regiment of a 1,000 dragoons. The infantry was made up of twelve regiments of 1,200 each. Finally, there were artillery and baggage trains.

Although many of the New Model soldiers were volunteers, at least half of them were reluctant conscripts. They set to work straight away, marching and drilling all day long. Any failure was severely punished. The soldiers wore fine red tunics which were to remain part of the British army's uniform until the introduction of khaki at the end of the nineteenth century. Unlike their predecessors, they were well paid and well fed.

The soldiers were armed with the usual weapons – the cavalry had swords and pistols, the dragoons swords and carbines, and the infantry pikes and muskets. However, there were twice as many musketeers as pikemen in the new regiments, and most of them were armed with flintlocks. The cavalry wore back and breast plates over buff coats of thick leather and strong helmets.

Below left Sir Thomas Fairfax, commander in chief of the New Model Army.

Above Ten figures supposed to represent the different soldiers of the New Model Army, from the fifer and drummer to the captain.

The soldiers who fought in this new army were brave, intelligent, and often dangerously outspoken men. "What were the lords of England," declared one, "but William the Conqueror's colonels." Such men had no respect for titles, and fought for an England where all men would be equal. They brought a new ruthlessness into the war, and some even vowed that if they met the King himself in battle, they would kill him without a second thought.

c

The battle of Naseby

Above Charles I on the battlefield at Naseby is stopped by Lord Carnath as he attempts to ride to the rescue of his infantry.

While the New Model Army was being thus organized and trained, the King had a marvellous opportunity to attack the Roundheads, but he failed to grasp it. Instead, the Royal Council made the fatal mistake of dividing up the Royalist army. Goring was sent with part of it to relieve Taunton, while the King sacked Leicester. This stirred the Roundheads to action, and General Fairfax set out to bring Charles to battle. The King was dangerously over-confident, and regarded the "New Noddle" as a joke.

The Cavaliers were brought to bay near the village of Naseby in the midst of fine rolling country. Charles had only 7,500 men, of whom 4,000 were cavalry. Rupert commanded the right wing, and Sir Marmaduke Langdale the left. The Roundheads numbered 14,000 – 7,000 infantry and 6,500 cavalry and dragoons. Cromwell commanded the right wing and Henry Ireton the left.

At half past ten, Rupert charged and shattered the Roundheads' left wing. Ireton was wounded and captured. But, once again, Rupert couldn't control his men who turned to plunder the baggage train before returning to the battle. A terrible sight met their eyes. Cromwell had meanwhile smashed Langdale's cavalry, and attacked the exposed flanks of the Royalist infantry.

Charles wanted to charge to their rescue with his horseguards, but Lord Carnath stopped him and, before the King knew what was happening, his whole reserve was galloping away.

Meanwhile, the heavily-outnumbered Royalist infantry had outdone themselves. Even though they were attacked on the right by Roundhead dragoons and on the left by Cromwell's cavalry, they managed to crash through the first line of the opposing infantry

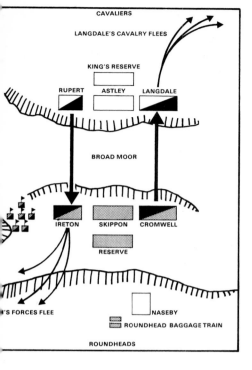

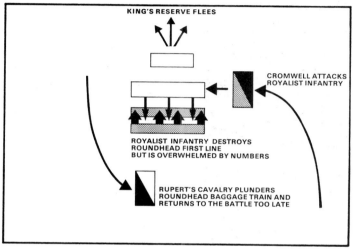

Above and right The two main stages of the battle of Naseby (1644), as first the Cavaliers and then the Roundheads gain the ascendency.

and attacked the reserve. However, they couldn't withstand such overwhelming odds for long. By the time Rupert returned to the field, they were finished and the battle was lost. As at Marston Moor, the Royalist infantry had fought with the greatest possible courage, but the cavalry fled with the enemy in hot pursuit.

The King escaped, but he had lost his main army. The Roundheads captured 5,000 soldiers, the royal artillery and all the King's private belongings. Then they disgraced themselves by massacring a hundred of the wretched women they found sheltering in the King's camp. Many more had their faces slashed and their noses split open. There was no room for mercy in the Roundheads' hearts.

The siege of Basing House

Although the Cavaliers' main army had been destroyed, they still held many fortified places. One of the strongest of these was Basing House, the home of the Marquis of Winchester. It had survived several sieges, and was garrisoned by determined men. The Marquis boasted that he could hold it for ever.

On 8th October, 1645, Cromwell arrived before the stronghold with four regiments of infantry and three of cavalry. He surveyed its formidable ram-

Above A propaganda cartoon, issued by the Parliamentarians, accusing the Cavaliers of atrocities. In fact, both sides during the Civil War were equally brutish. When they captured Basing House, the Roundheads butchered more than three hundred people, including many civilians.

parts with misgiving – he admitted himself that siege warfare was not one of his strong points. Nevertheless he sited his guns with skill and, for six whole days, the fortifications were relentlessly pounded by a hurricane of shot. On the seventh, a wide breach was opened in the walls, and Cromwell announced that there would be a general assault the following day.

The next morning, Cromwell's Ironsides stormed through the breach with incredible ferocity. In spite of the accurate fire of the defenders, they placed their scaling ladders against the walls and swarmed up and over the parapets. In the bitter hand to hand fighting that followed three hundred people were butchered. Civilian refugees as well as Cavaliers were cut down. One of those killed was Robbins the Player, a professional comedian who had once delighted London audiences with his merry quips. A young woman was run through and left dying when she tried to save her father, a clergyman, from the frenzied Roundheads.

Fortunately, the eyes of the attackers soon fell upon the many treasures that filled the house. The greedy soldiers stopped killing, and started looting instead. Silver and gold plate, rich wall hangings, jewels and furniture were all carried off. When one soldier boasted that he had found three bags of silver, his less fortunate comrades immediately turned on him, and stripped him of his booty. By the end of the day, he had only half-a-crown ($12\frac{1}{2}$ p.) left.

Once the troops had withdrawn from the house, the remaining goods were auctioned off to the highest bidder. The sale went on for days. The fall of Basing House opened up the trade routes between London and the West Country. Once again, lines of pack mules could trudge their weary way to the capital loaded down with sacks of wool.

The end of the first civil war

Rupert couldn't make the King understand how serious the defeat at Naseby had been. Charles insisted: "I am nowise disheartened by our late misfortune. I hope shortly to recover my late loss with advantage."

Charles joined the incompetent Goring and the western army. Fairfax followed him and forced the Cavaliers to give battle. By this time, the New Model was a fine and disciplined army, and it soon drove the Cavaliers from the field. What had begun as an orderly retreat quickly turned into a rout. Next, the New Model Army appeared before the walls of Bristol. Since it was impossible for him to defend the sprawling city with only 2,000 men, Rupert surrendered. Charles was furious, and when the Prince urged him to make peace, he expelled him from his Council.

Meanwhile, the Roundheads took no chances. Fairfax led his men through the January snows into Devonshire, and defeated Sir Ralph Hopton at Torrington. The last battle of the war was fought at Stow-in-the-Wold on 21st March, 1646. On surrendering, the old Cavalier, Lord Astley, muttered: "You have done your work boys; you may go play, unless you fall out among yourselves."

For some time, the King negotiated with all and sundry but without success. Then he surrendered to the Scots. Now that he was no longer surrounded by smooth tongued courtiers, Charles soon learned how unpopular he was. There followed the most unpleasant period of his life, as everyone badgered him to accept the reformed church he loathed. When the King refused to submit to their terms, the Scots handed him over to the English. The war was ended, but could the peace last?

Opposite Royalist infantry hold back the Roundhead enemy while their wounded commander escapes from the field of battle. By the end of the first civil war, the Cavaliers were too weak and too demoralized to stand up to the discipline of the New Model Army.

4. The impossible peace

Charles was taken to Holmby House in North-
amptonshire, while the Roundheads quarrelled
among themselves. Parliament wanted to demobilize
most of the army, but the soldiers refused to agree.

Oliver Cromwell meanwhile ordered a certain
Cornet Joyce to guard the King. When Charles asked
to see his commission or warrant, Joyce pointed to his
troops. The King smiled and agreed: "It is as fair a

Above This contemporary
cartoon shows King Charles
imprisoned on the Isle of
Wight. While he was there,
the King plotted continuously
for his escape and this is
reflected in the cartoon, where
the name of the island has
been changed to the Isle of
"Wait."

56

commission and as well-written as I have seen a commission in my life."

Charles was later moved to Hampton Court, near London, and there the generals tried to persuade him to accept a modified constitution. The King continued to refuse, hoping that his enemies would eventually fall out among themselves. The ordinary soldiers who had fought for a new society were angry at all this manoeuvring. Thomas Rainborough spoke for most of them when he said: "I think that the poorest that is in England has a life to live as well as the greatest He." These hopes, however, weren't shared by the generals, who wanted to preserve the old society with its rigid class structure.

While the soldiers were arguing among themselves, Charles escaped from Hampton Court and took refuge in Carisbrooke Castle, on the Isle of Wight. Many soldiers blamed Cromwell for this escapade, and some even plotted to murder him. When he learned about this, Cromwell went to inspect the mutinous regiments with a gleaming sword in his hand and a grim look on his face – but just the sight of "Old Ironsides" was enough to crush the mutiny.

Although the Governor of the Isle of Wight arrested him, Charles continued to negotiate with his enemies. Finally, he signed the Engagement, a treaty by which he agreed to set up a Presbyterian Church in England provided the Scots would put him back on the throne. So the Scots invaded England.

Charles had condemned the country to another civil war. The angry Roundheads vowed: "If ever the Lord bring us back in peace, we shall call Charles Stuart, that man of blood, to account for all that blood he has shed."

The second civil war

To make matters worse, discontented men all over Britain rose in revolt, and particularly in South Wales. Cromwell was sent off with two cavalry regiments and three of infantry to recapture Pembroke from the rebels. On the way there, one of his ships was sunk in the Bristol Channel, and with it most of his guns, so that he had to rely on a new kind of large mortar. It was six weeks before the garrison surrendered and Cromwell was able to move north again.

Meanwhile, risings in Kent and Essex kept Fairfax fully occupied until the end of August. This meant that when the Scots crossed the border on 8th July, it was up to Cromwell and not to his commander-in-chief to defend England against them. The Scots under the Duke of Hamilton joined Sir Marmaduke Langdale and his northerners and then marched south to Preston. Here, Cromwell fell upon them even before they knew he was in the vicinity.

Langdale with 3,000 infantry and 600 cavalry found himself faced by 4,000 infantry and 2,500 cavalry. In torrential rain, the old Cavalier took up position in some small fenced fields. Although Cromwell easily outflanked his enemy, the Ironsides found it difficult to dislodge the Royalist soldiers from the hedgerows. Langdale and his men resisted bravely for four hours before numbers told, and they were forced to retreat into the town. The Royalist reserves were wiped out. Only Hamilton and a few of the cavalry managed to escape by swimming across the River Ribble. A thousand men were killed and 4,000 Cavaliers captured. Within a few days, the rest of the Scots army was rounded up and forced to surrender.

Cromwell had no difficulty in arranging terms with the Scots. In mid-October, he was able to return

to England, and soon had captured the Cavalier stronghold of Pontefract. The Second Civil War was over. Even at this late date, however, Charles was still negotiating with Parliament; and the horrified soldiers feared lest once again the King should escape the consequences of his actions.

Above The Scots pursued by Cromwell's Ironsides after the battle of Preston (1648). A few of them managed to escape by swimming across the river, but over a thousand were killed.

A court to try the King

The army and parliament were at loggerheads. The soldiers wanted a new constitution, while the Presbyterian members of parliament determined to come to an agreement with the King, and dismiss the army. On 6th December, 1648, Colonel Pride marched down to the House of Commons with a body of musketeers and stopped a hundred Presbyterian members of parliament from taking their seats. All that remained now of the Long Parliament

Above King Charles I at his trial (20th–27th January, 1649). During his trial, the King lost his painful stammer, and spoke clearly and with dignity.

was a mere "Rump" of some 45 to 50 members.

Cromwell himself was convinced that further negotiations with Charles were impractical. If Charles were imprisoned, he would immediately become the focus for every discontented group in England. If he were deposed and banished, he would be sure to return at the head of a foreign army. There was nothing for it but to put him on trial for his crimes. On 6th January, 1649, the Rump Parliament passed an ordinance setting up a high court of justice to try the King, and when the House of Lords refused to agree to this, it was abolished.

But Charles, at this the lowest point of his fortunes, found a new strength. Indeed, he was a different man – his painful stammer disappeared, and he spoke clearly and well. When he heard himself referred to as a traitor, he laughed outright. He refused to recognize the authority of the court and, as he was led away by his guards, the spectators shouted: "God save the King!" On his next visit, he again refused to plead, saying: "It is not my case alone, it is the freedom and liberty of the people of England that are on trial." In fury, one of the guards spat in the King's face. Charles said gently: "God has justice in store both for you and for me."

On 27th January, the trial was brought to an end. Charles wasn't even allowed to speak in his own defence. He was sentenced to death and bundled out of the hall. His voice was drowned by the soldiers' shouts of "Justice!" and "Execution!" Some soldiers puffed tobacco smoke into his face. "Poor souls," said he. "For sixpence, they would do the same for their commanders."

Many people were shocked by the verdict. The ordinary people wept openly in the streeets. Yet what other answer was there?

Cruel necessity

Charles received the news of his death sentence calmly. Indeed, he was almost gay. When his two youngest children, Princess Elizabeth and Henry, Duke of Gloucester, were brought before him, he took them on his knees and comforted them. "He wished me," wrote Princess Elizabeth later, "not to grieve or torment myself for him, for that would be a glorious death he should die, it being for the laws and liberties of this land, and for maintaining the true Protestant religion."

The day of the execution, Tuesday 30th January, 1649, dawned cold and grey. Charles rose early and dressed with care. He wore an extra shirt to make sure he wouldn't shiver, for he didn't want people to think he was afraid.

After receiving Holy Communion, he walked through the bitter cold to the Palace of Whitehall where he had to delay for several hours. At half past one, he passed through lines of spectators on his way to the Banqueting Hall. On the black-draped scaffold stood two masked executioners.

The King spoke a few words. "I am the martyr of the people," he said. After tucking his long hair inside a white satin cap, he placed his head on the block and said a few simple prayers. Then he stretched out his arms, and the axe fell. The executioner held up the severed head for all to see, and a low moan escaped from those spectators who had come to watch the deed. Then silent ranks of cavalry rode into the crowd, forcing the people away from the scaffold.

Both men and women paid well for the privilege of queueing up to dip their handkerchiefs in the King's blood, and to snip off locks of his hair. Then the body was embalmed and the head sewn back onto the trunk. As the King was carried to his last resting place in St. George's Chapel, Windsor, it started to snow. By the time the procession reached its destination, the black coffin had turned white, the colour of innocence. "So went the white King to his grave, in the forty-eighth year of his life and the twenty-second year and tenth month of his reign."

Exploits at sea

In the summer of 1648, part of the Roundhead navy mutinied and sailed across to Holland where Prince Rupert took command. His mother pawned her jewels so that he could equip this "royal fleet" with provisions.

The Prince sailed to Ireland in January, 1649, and settled near Kinsale. From there, he ran arms and supplies across to the Royalists still left in England until the Roundhead admiral, Robert Blake, trapped him in Kinsale. In November, Rupert escaped during a violent storm and made his way to Portugal, capturing four more ships on the way. When Blake arrived off Lisbon, hot in pursuit, King John of Portugal refused to order Rupert out of the sheltering waters of the River Tagus. Blake then tried to kidnap the Prince while he was out hunting, and Rupert retaliated by placing a time-bomb on board one of Blake's ships.

In the end, Rupert managed to slip away during rough weather and entered the Mediterranean. For a time, he sailed up and down the Spanish coast, raiding and capturing ships, until Blake destroyed part of his fleet off Carthagena. In spite of this setback, Rupert reached Toulon in safety. There, he sold off the ships he had captured, and refitted his own fleet.

Next, the Prince dodged the Roundheads who were pursuing him, and sailed down the coast of Africa to Gambia, where he captured four more richly-laden prizes. Then he set out across the Atlantic. Although his ships were leaky and ill-equipped, he made the perilous crossing safely and was able to land on the island of St. Lucia. There the Cavaliers feasted on wild boar and delicious tropical fruits.

Gradually, they made their way north, harassing Roundhead shipping until they were caught by a hurricane in the rocky passage between the Virgin and the Leeward Islands. During the storm, Rupert's brother's ship sank with all hands. Rupert was heartbroken, and sailed immediately for home in his sole surviving vessel. On reaching the mouth of the River Loire, in France, his luck finally ran out, and the ship went aground.

After three years at sea, Rupert hadn't much to show for all his efforts except an undying reputation for courage.

Opposite A woodcut taken from a book published in 1649, showing "a great and bloody fight at sea between five men-of-war belonging to the parliament of England, and a squadron of Prince Rupert's fleet."

Below left The route followed by Prince Rupert during his exploits at sea (1649–52).

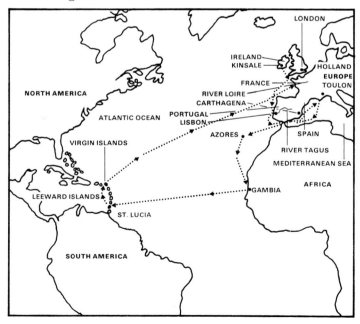

5. The Commonwealth

Meanwhile, the first task that faced the new republic was the pacification of Ireland. The Irish, both Catholic and Protestant, were united in horror at the execution of the King. By midsummer, only Dublin and Londonderry remained loyal to the new republic, and Cromwell was appointed to lead an expeditionary force to deal with the rebellion.

As soon as he arrived in Ireland, Cromwell moved against the well-fortified town of Drogheda. His siege train opened fire on 10th September, 1649, and

pounded the walls for two days. Late on the second day, Cromwell launched a general assault. Twice the Roundheads were repulsed but at the third attempt they broke through, led by Cromwell in person.

No quarter was given. Fire and sword swept through the city. The rebel commander was battered to death with his own wooden leg. Some eighty people who took refuge in the steeple of St. Peter's Church were burned to death. The massacre continued throughout the night and the following day. Yet Cromwell felt that this was only the "righteous judgement of God upon these barbarous wretches."

Next, Cromwell moved south to Wexford. The soldiers in the castle garrison surrendered, but the citizens fought on. A brief but bloody battle took place in the narrow streets, and some 2,000 soldiers and citizens perished. This time Cromwell wasn't responsible for the massacre, but he gloried in it all the same. In his view, the Irish were an inferior breed of men.

For a time, the Roundheads made easy progress. Then new and more terrible enemies got to work among their ranks. Malaria, dysentery and spotted fever struck them down with greater fury than ever the Irish had. Early in 1650, Cromwell captured Kilkenny and Clonmel, but at great cost. Two thousand Roundheads fell at Clonmel during a single assault.

At this point, Cromwell returned to England, and a hero's welcome. The backbone of Irish resistance had been broken, although the Irish did not actually admit defeat until 1652. Cromwell's Irish campaign has never been forgotten or forgiven. It remains the greatest stain on this great soldier's record.

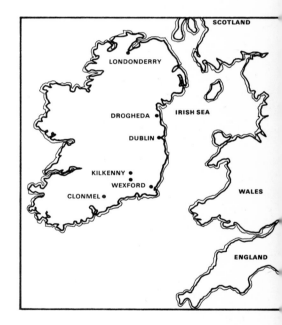

Above A map of Ireland, showing the main areas of conflict
Opposite The Roundheads behaved with extreme brutality in Ireland, and left behind them a wake of burned villages and battered bodies.

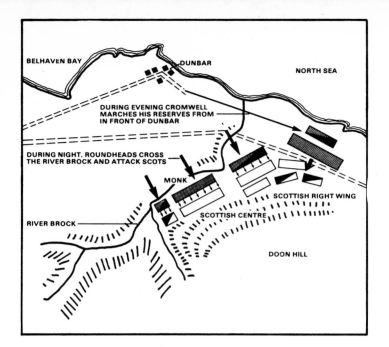

Inside map:
BELHAVEN BAY
DUNBAR
NORTH SEA
DURING EVENING CROMWELL MARCHES HIS RESERVES FROM IN FRONT OF DUNBAR
DURING NIGHT, ROUNDHEADS CROSS THE RIVER BROCK AND ATTACK SCOTS
MONK
SCOTTISH RIGHT WING
SCOTTISH CENTRE
RIVER BROCK
DOON HILL

Opposite Cromwell preaches to his troops before the battle of Dunbar (1650). Cromwell was a deeply religious man, and used to read from the Bible before and after every battle.

Left Plan of the battle of Dunbar, showing how Cromwell marched his reserves from in front of the town to an unexpected position beyond the Scottish right wing.

The battle of Dunbar

The execution of Charles I stirred the Scots to fury, and soon they had proclaimed his son King Charles II. When the new King arrived in Scotland, war between the two countries became inevitable.

Since Fairfax refused to lead the New Model Army against his old allies, Cromwell was appointed commander-in-chief in his place. In July, 1650, he set out with 10,500 infantry and 5,500 cavalry to face a formidable Scots army, led by the experienced David Leslie. Cromwell advanced first on Edinburgh, hoping thus to bring the Scots to battle. Sensibly, however, the Scots defended themselves behind earthworks which were impregnable to an army lacking siege guns. The English achieved nothing and were forced to retreat to Dunbar, with the Scots harrying their every step.

All that Cromwell could do was to defend Dunbar, and wait for the English fleet to rescue him. Leslie, on his part, was determined that the Roundheads shouldn't escape. So the Scots left their impregnable position in the hills and descended onto the cramped

slopes above the coastal plain. As Cromwell watched them, he worked out a masterly plan. During the night, he moved his reserves from in front of the town across the River Brock to a position beyond the Scots' right wing. While this manoeuvre was being accomplished in the bitter cold, the English guns on the right opened fire. In the pale moonlight, the Roundheads attacked the Scottish left wing. Shortly afterwards, the English centre crossed the stream and engaged its opposite number. The English, however, were repulsed until Cromwell and his men suddenly came in to attack the unsuspecting Scots from the right.

In the chaos that followed, the Scots were pushed back for three-quarters of a mile. One of the soldiers who took part wrote: "I never beheld a more terrible charge of foot." Encouraged by their comrades' success, the English centre and right wing returned to the attack and completed the rout. The Scots left three thousand dead on the battlefield. The English escaped with only twenty killed.

The Scottish campaign

Below right A map of Scotland. The Scots were deeply shocked by the execution of Charles I, and proclaimed his son King Charles II.

Below Charles II is crowned in the small church at Scone, on 1st January, 1651.

During the autumn and winter of 1650, the Scots fought with even greater courage and skill than before, and Cromwell made little progress against them. Edinburgh Castle proved a great stumbling block. Derbyshire miners were brought north to undermine its solid foundations but with little success. However, the castle was mercilessly battered by Cromwell's great mortars until the governor eventually surrendered on 24th December.

Meanwhile, Charles II was beginning to display

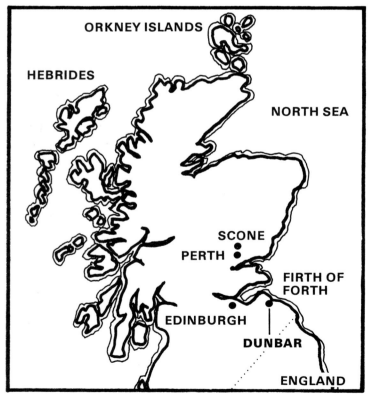

some of the powers of leadership for which he later became famous. He charmed the proud and difficult highlanders, Protestant and Catholic alike. And, on 1st January, 1651, he was crowned King in the church at Scone.

For the first six months of 1651, the Scottish general Leslie countered with masterly skill all the English attempts to bring him to battle. In the end, all the English had to show for half a year's hard campaigning were a few castles and a sick general. Since February, Cromwell had been near to death – he suffered from recurring bouts of malaria throughout his life. By the end of June, however, he was sufficiently recovered to get back into the saddle.

Knowing that his army couldn't stand another cruel Scottish winter, Cromwell worked out a daring plan. He decided to cross the Firth of Forth, and force the Scots to choose between giving battle, retiring into the Western Highlands, or making a run for England.

Major-General Lambert landed 4,000 men on the northern shore of the Firth before the Scots had realized what was happening. When they did attack the English bridgehead, they were utterly defeated. By a series of brilliant manoeuvres, Cromwell managed to gain complete control of the Firth and, on 2nd August, he forced the important town of Perth to surrender.

At this point, Leslie wanted to try and cut Cromwell's communications with England, but the young King and his hot-headed Cavaliers insisted on marching into England and raising the country for the royal cause. So 20,000 Scots, many of them wild highlanders, left Stirling and tramped south into England. Cromwell's trap was sprung.

Worcester

The young King was disappointed in his hopes. The English didn't rise and join him. Instead, the further south he marched, the more Scots deserted his banner. Meanwhile, Cromwell was marching at top speed through the eastern counties. Gradually their routes converged. On 22nd August, 1652, 16,000 footsore and weary Scotsmen arrived before Worcester. Charles occupied the city and prepared to fight for his life and his cause. Meanwhile, Cromwell collected his forces and moved in for the kill.

The third day of September dawned bright and cloudless. At two o'clock in the afternoon, Lieutenant-General Fleetwood, Cromwell's second-in-command, opened the battle by attacking the line of the River Teme, which was defended by three Scottish regiments. The Scots defenders fought with such spirit that Cromwell was forced to send his reserve in to Fleetwood's aid. Meanwhile Cromwell himself advanced against the city's eastern defences.

As he watched from the tower of the cathedral, Charles realized that his only hope of victory was to

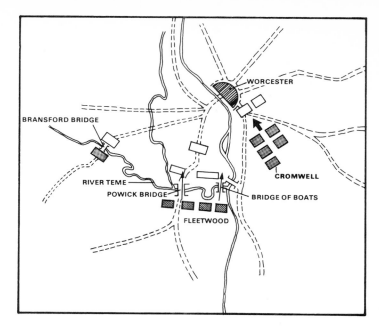

Opposite The routes followed respectively by Charles II and Cromwell during their long march south from Scotland.

Right Plan of the battle of Worcester (1651). Although the Scots fought with great bravery, they were eventually overrun by the superior numbers of Cromwell's troops.

Below left After his defeat at Worcester, Charles was a wanted man, with a price on his head. This picture shows him exchanging clothes with a shepherd in an attempt at disguise.

destroy one or other arm of the divided Roundhead army. He ordered the royal guns to give him cover, and then led a wild cavalry attack on Cromwell's position. For three hours the contest swayed back and forth, until sheer weight of numbers told, and the Scots retreated into the city.

Meanwhile, Fleetwood had succeeded in crossing the River Teme over a bridge of boats, and fought his way to the southern gate of the city. A bitter struggle took place in the streets of Worcester. The Scots knew that no quarter would be given so they fought on with desperate courage. "As stiff a contest for four or five hours as I have ever seen," confessed Cromwell. The Roundheads captured 10,000 Scots, including all their main leaders except for the King himself.

Charles escaped from Worcester with a price on his head. A reward of £1,000 was offered for information leading to his arrest. All England was on the look out for "Charles Stuart, a long dark man, above two yards high."

D

Charles's escape

As night fell on 3rd September, 1652, Charles and a small band of fugitives sped through the wooded valleys north of Worcester. At last they found refuge in a cottage belonging to the Penderels, a family of poor woodcutters. Here Charles changed into farm-labourer's clothes, and had his long hair cropped short.

The next day was spent sleeping in the woods, and the night trudging across country. Charles found it

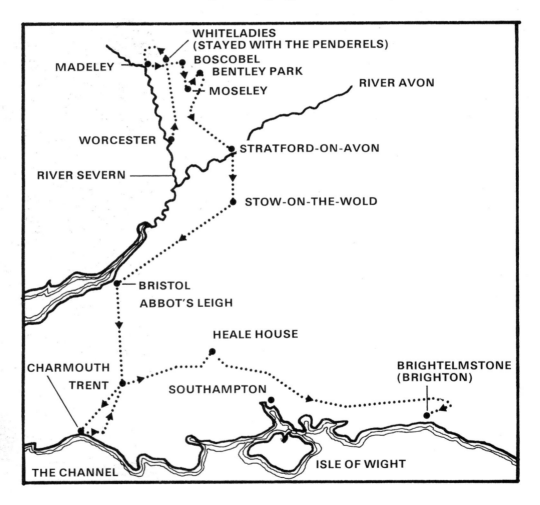

hard going. His feet were soon rubbed raw so he walked barefoot. At Madeley, he hid in a hayloft. The following night he walked to Boscobel, where Joan Penderel bandaged his feet. As Cromwell's troopers were searching the surrounding woods, the King spent two days hidden in a huge oak tree.

He still couldn't walk, so the Penderels found him an old mill horse on which to ride to Moseley. While he was there, a company of militia arrived and searched the house, but Charles was safely hidden away in a priest's hole. The King's next stop was Bentley Park where he disguised himself as a servant, in a suit and cloak of sober grey, and a tall black hat. For a week, he rode pillion with Jane Lane until they reached Trent, where Frank Wyndham took over.

Wyndham conducted Charles to Charmouth, where a boat was supposed to be waiting to carry him over to France. The boat failed to arrive, and the King moved on to Bridgport. This was just as well since Charles had been recognized in Charmouth and, soon after he left, a troop of horse arrived to arrest him.

Unaware of his narrow escape, Charles stayed the night at a little inn in Broadwindsor. No sooner was he in bed than a company of soldiers arrived and demanded lodgings for the night. Next morning, the unsuspecting soldiers marched away, and Charles returned to Trent. He remained there for another week.

Then he moved on to Heale, where a widow called Mrs. Hyde hid him in her house. From Heale the King travelled to Brighton. There the brig, *The Surprise,* was waiting to carry him to safety.

At high tide on the 14th October, 1652, the King sailed away from England, vowing that one day he would return to claim his own.

Opposite The route of Charles's escape after the battle of Worcester.

Below The story of Charles's escape soon became legendary, and all over the south of England there are oak trees where he is supposed to have hidden, and inns where he is supposed to have stayed.

England under Cromwell

Now that the Irish and the Scots had been pacified, all should have been well for the new English republic, but it wasn't. Parliament and the army couldn't agree. The army wanted parliament to be dissolved and to hold new elections, while the Parliamentarians called for the demobilization of the army. The conflict came to a head in April, 1653, when the army submitted a scheme for a new system of government.

The Rump Parliament had no intention of losing its powers, and proceeded to discuss a bill to continue its existence. When Cromwell heard about this, he collected together a group of musketeers and marched down to the House of Commons. For a few minutes he listened to the debate, then he rose and roared: "It is not fit that you should sit as a parliament any longer." When the members began to protest, he shouted: "I will put an end to your prating. You are no parliament." He signalled to Major-General Harrison, and the musketeers filed into the chamber. Without ceremony, the members were bundled out, and the doors locked. Later, some witty person pinned a notice to the door, saying: "This House to let unfurnished."

Cromwell was determined to work out a better constitution. First he followed the advice of Major-General Harrison, and called together a parliament of "Saints," representatives nominated by the independent churches in each county. But as soon as they met, they began to quarrel. On 12th December, 1653, the moderate majority resigned their powers. Cromwell had to think again.

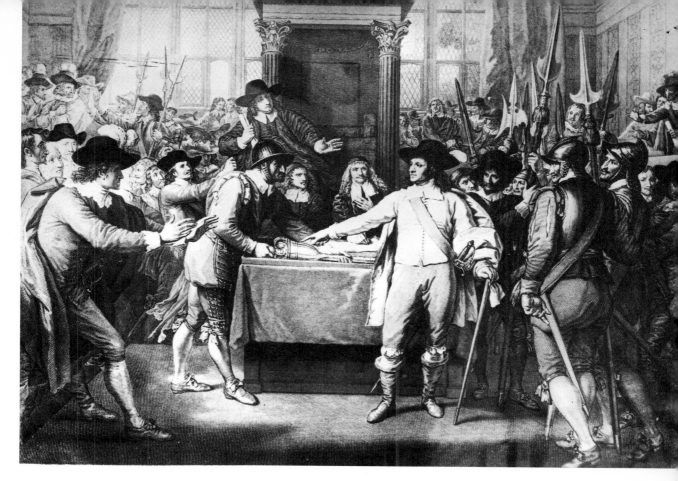

Above Cromwell found parliament no easier to deal with than had Charles I, and he was eventually forced to dissolve it. This picture shows him removing the mace, the symbol of authority, on 20th April, 1653.

This time, he accepted a constitution drawn up by Major-General Lambert, The Instrument of Government. By this, Cromwell became Lord Protector, and ruled Britain with the help of a Council of State and a parliament. Some good work was done under this scheme. England, Scotland and Ireland were united. The legal system was simplified. Duelling was forbidden, and drunkenness and swearing severely punished.

However, when the first Protectorate parliament met in September, 1654, the old tensions reappeared. The members tried to modify the constitution, and Cromwell dissolved parliament. Nothing much had changed since the days of Charles I.

Left When Cromwell became Protector, he assumed responsibility for the whole country. This cartoon, called "Cromwell's Car," shows him holding liberty and the Church in balance at the point of a sword, while the fair kingdoms of England, Scotland and Ireland are asleep. The chariot he is riding has just run over Charles I, whose head is cut off.

Opposite A map showing England divided up into the different major-generalships which Cromwell established in order to maintain law and order (1655).

The Sealed Knot

Once more, Cromwell found himself sole ruler of England. The country seethed with discontent. Most serious of all, the Cavaliers were plotting to restore the King. A secret society known as the Sealed Knot was formed to organize risings in the north, the midlands and the west. But so many people were involved in it that it became impossible to keep the enterprise secret. John Thurloe, Cromwell's chief secretary, had set up an efficient secret service. His agents attended the conspirators' meetings and soon Cromwell knew as much about their plans as the conspirators themselves.

In the event, there was only one small rising, in the West Country. On 12th March, 1655, Colonel John Penruddock marched into Salisbury with 200 men. He broke open the gaols, and proclaimed Charles II as King. Then he continued through Blandford, Shaftesbury and Sherbourne. By this time, Major-General Desborough was hot on his trail. The Roundheads caught up with their prey at South Molton in Devon. Fierce street fighting took place. The Cavaliers defended themselves courageously for some time but, in the end, most of them surrendered and were taken prisoner to Exeter.

Cromwell was surprisingly merciful. Less than a third of those captured were brought to trial. Only 39 of them were sentenced to death, and most were reprieved at the last minute. Penruddock, however, was beheaded, and died bravely.

Next, Cromwell divided England into several separate districts, each one under the control of a major-general. The major-generals commanded a force of cavalry, as well as the local militia. They were very unpopular and were vigorously condemned.

The rising in the West Country had shown that Cromwell was only safe while he had the support of the army. In 1656, parliament introduced yet another constitution, the Humble Petition and Advice, by which Cromwell was given the right to name his successor, and parliament was divided into an upper and a lower house. This constitution was a compromise – many people had wanted Cromwell to become King, but the soldiers had opposed the idea. They feared that once crowned, Cromwell would have no further need of them.

THE MAJOR-GENERALS
1. JOHN LAMBERT —YORKSHIRE AND THE NORTH.
2. CHARLES WORSLEY —LANCS, CHESHIRE AND STAFFS.
3. EDWARD WHALLEY —LINCS, LEICS, DERBY, NOTTS AND WARWICK.
4. JAMES BERRY —WORCS, HEREFORD, MONMOUTH, SHROPSHIRE AND WALES.
5. WILLIAM BOTELER —BEDS, HUNTS, RUTLAND AND NORTHANTS.
6. CHARLES FLEETWOOD—OXFORD, BUCKS, HERTS, ESSEX, NORFOLK AND SUFFOLK.
7. PHILLIP SKIPPON —LONDON AND MIDDLESEX.
   & JOHN BARKSTEAD
8. JOHN DESBOROUGH —THE WEST COUNTRY.
9. WILLIAM GOFFE —SUSSEX, HANTS AND BERKS.
10. THOMAS KELSEY —KENT AND SURREY.

The Ironsides abroad

When Cromwell came to power, he had hoped to keep out of the wars that were then ravaging Europe. But when English merchantmen were repeatedly attacked in the Mediterranean, he decided to dispatch a fleet under Admiral Robert Blake to deal with the situation.

Once in the Mediterranean, Blake sailed around destroying Spanish, French and Italian shipping. He also dealt firmly with the Barbary pirates who had been terrorizing the shores of Europe for many years. When the Bey of Tunis refused to hand over his English captives, Blake sailed straight into the harbour of Porto Farina, bombarded the fortifications and destroyed the Bey's fleet. After this, the Bey of Algiers was happy to surrender his prisoners without further argument.

Meanwhile, Admiral Penn and General Venables sailed to the West Indies with instructions to attack the Spanish empire. Everything went wrong from the start. 2,500 poor-quality troops invaded the island of Hispaniola in January, 1655. But they

Below The defeat of the Dutch fleet by Admiral Robert Blake. The exploits at sea of Blake and his men made the Commonwealth into the greatest naval power in the world.

couldn't cope with the jungles and the difficult terrain, and had to be withdrawn. Next month, they managed to capture the barren island of Jamaica, so at least they had something to show for all the money they had spent. But when they reached home, Penn and Venables were imprisoned for returning without orders.

By this time, England was at war with Spain. Cromwell had been warned by Blake that the fleet was in bad condition, so he allowed the admiral a free hand in reorganizing it. Soon, it was ready for action. Throughout 1656, the Spanish coast was blockaded by English squadrons. On 8th September, eight Spanish treasure ships returning laden from America were sighted near Cadiz. After a fiercely-fought battle, four ships worth two million pounds were sunk, and another worth £600,000 was captured.

Blake's last and greatest exploit took place in the Canary Islands. On 20th April, 1657, he led his navy into the harbour of Santa Cruz in Teneriffe, where the Spanish treasure fleet had taken refuge. The English fleet challenged at once the guns of the galleons and the batteries on shore, and emerged victorious. All sixteen Spanish vessels were sunk, while the English escaped without losing a single ship. But the great admiral was worn out. He survived the long journey home, and died as his ships entered Plymouth Sound.

Cromwell's "Generals-at-Sea," as his admirals were called, made Britain the greatest naval power in the world.

The battle of the Dunes

After their defeat in the Civil War, many Cavaliers fled abroad and joined the armies of France or Spain. One such exile was Charles II's younger brother, James, Duke of York, who between 1652 and 1655 served with such distinction in the French army that he was almost made a Marshal of France — a very high honour. But then Cromwell signed a treaty of alliance with France in October, 1655, and the Duke was forced to resign his French commission and seek employment elsewhere, this time in Spain.

In 1657, as a result of the treaty of alliance, 6,000 Roundhead soldiers landed at Boulogne and joined the French army under Marshal Turenne, who were fighting the Spanish. During their first campaign, they laid siege to a number of towns in the Spanish Netherlands (modern Belgium). In 1658, Turenne laid siege to Dunkirk, a Spanish-held stronghold just north of Calais. A Spanish army of 14,000 men was sent to relieve it, with James, Duke of York, in command of the right wing. As soon as the English redcoats saw the enemy, they gave a great cheer and dashed up the sandhills, forcing James's infantry to give ground. Hoping to save the situation, the Duke led his cavalry in a fierce charge against the English. But half his men were shot down by the English musketeers before they reached their lines. The Duke himself fought gallantly, but was only saved from serious injury by the strength and quality of his armour.

While the rest of the Spanish army retreated, James charged again. This time, he was completely surrounded by the English, but managed to bluff his way out of trouble by pretending to be a French

Right This contemporary woodcut shows the body of Oliver Cromwell lying in state at Somerset House. His death on 3rd September, 1658, left the country without a real leader.

Below The French Marshal Turenne leads his troops against the Spanish at the battle of the Dunes (1658). Turenne later gave credit for his victory to Cromwell's Ironsides, and Dunkirk was handed over to the English as a token of French gratitude.

officer. Later Marshal Turenne gave credit for his victory at the battle of the Dunes to the gallantry of Cromwell's Ironsides, and Dunkirk was handed over to the English as a token of French gratitude.

At this point, however, the Protector fell ill. He died on 3rd September, 1658, the anniversary of the battles of Dunbar and Worcester. John Milton wrote of him: "He was a soldier disciplined to perfection in the knowledge of himself. He had either extinguished or by habit had learned to subdue the whole host of vain hopes, fears, and passions, which infest the soul."

6. The end of the Commonwealth

Cromwell's death destroyed the system of government he had struggled to create. Instead of appointing one of his generals, or his able son Henry, as his successor, he chose his weak eldest son, Richard.

In January, 1659, Richard summoned his first parliament. But he was no more successful than his father at controlling this turbulent body. The Generals, led by Major-General Lambert, a vain, ambitious man, soon forced Richard to dissolve parliament and recall the Rump. Very sensibly, Richard then resigned.

Encouraged by these disorders, groups of Presbyterians led by Sir George Booth rose in revolt in

Gloucestershire and Cheshire, demanding the restoration of the King. This threat temporarily united the generals, and Lambert was sent north to deal with the rising. On 23rd August, he faced Booth, only to find that the Royalists melted away, "without any loss other than that of reputation."

Flushed with this success, the generals tried to force parliament to grant their demands, but the old Republicans wouldn't give in. So, just as Cromwell had done, Lambert gathered together a company of musketeers, marched on Westminster, and expelled the Rump.

When the news of this outrage reached Scotland, General George Monk decided it was time to restore order. Monk was a man of honour. Disgusted by the behaviour of his brother officers, he announced that he would free England from "the intolerable slavery of a sword government."

While Monk was preparing to march south, Lambert arrived in York with some 6,000 troops. It seemed that renewed civil war was inevitable. But while the two sides were probing each other's weaknesses, both the navy and the army in Ireland announced that they supported parliament.

On New Year's Day, 1660, Monk marched through the ice and snow into England. Lambert's troops deserted him, and he threw himself on the mercy of parliament. England's future lay in the capable hands of General George Monk.

The restoration

Charles II watched these events at a distance, with interest but with little hope. In 1659, Monk had declared: "As to the Cavaliers' interest, I think I may modestly aver it hath no greater enemy in the three nations than myself." On 3rd February, 1660, Monk entered London and received the thanks of the grateful Rump. As a reward for his services, he was appointed commander-in-chief of the army, which made him the most powerful man in Britain.

But Monk faced a serious situation. The City of London refused to pay any more taxes until the Rump held by-elections to fill up its vacancies. Monk was ordered to arrest certain leading citizens, and to pull down the gates to the city. He obeyed reluctantly. Like Cromwell and Lambert before him, he soon realized that the Rump was impossible. Instead of expelling its members, however, he insisted that they should recall their excluded colleagues. London rejoiced. Samuel Pepys recorded: "It was a pleasant sight to see the city from one end to another with a glory about it, so high was the light of the bonfires, . . . and the bells rang everywhere."

Left Monk's rapturous reception in the City of London after he had insisted that the members of the Rump should recall all their excluded colleagues, and hold new elections.

At last, the Long Parliament dissolved itself, and held a general election. Meanwhile, Monk opened negotiations with Charles II. But, before the King could be restored, he had to make it clear that he accepted the reforms made in 1641. To convince the doubtful, Charles issued the Declaration of Breda, by which he pardoned everyone who had fought against him except for those whom parliament might exclude. He promised that no one would be persecuted because of their religion. The army was to be paid all the money it was due, and any claims to land were to be settled by parliament rather than by him. The new parliament declared itself satisfied with these assurances, and invited the King to return.

The fleet under Admiral Montagu sailed over to Holland and collected the King. The fleet anchored off Dover on 25th May, 1660. Everywhere Charles went on his triumphal progress to London, he was met with cheering crowds. On one occasion, the King turned to his friends with a wicked smile and said: "It must be my own fault that I've been absent so long, for everybody I see protests he has always wished for my return."

Right Charles II lands at Dover, and is greeted by his loyal subjects (26th May, 1660). Everywhere the King went on his triumphal progress to London, he was met by cheering crowds.

The legacy

But twenty years of bitter fighting cannot be forgotten
overnight. On 4th December, 1660, parliament
ordered the bodies of Oliver Cromwell and several
others to be dug up, drawn through the streets to the
public gallows, and hanged for their part in the
execution of Charles I. This gruesome ceremony was
carried out on the twelfth anniversary of Charles's
death. Later, the heads of the corpses were cut off
and displayed on poles outside Westminster Hall.
Next, parliament turned on the living. Twenty-nine

people were tried for the murder of Charles I. All of them were found guilty, but only ten were executed. The bravest of them all was Major-General Harrison. "Not a tear, wife," he said. "What hurt have they done me, to send me so soon to Heaven?"

Although Charles II had promised his people freedom of worship, the Anglicans in parliament were determined to be revenged upon the Puritans for what they had suffered during the Commonwealth period. Soon they had passed a series of acts, the Clarendon Code, which prevented the Puritans from taking part in public life.

Reluctantly, Charles was forced to disband Cromwell's magnificent army. Only two infantry regiments, the Coldstream and the Grenadier Guards, and two of cavalry, the Life Guards and the famous Horse Guards, were retained to become the nucleus of any future regular army. The navy continued to be Charles's pride and joy. Although lack of money led to a decline in its standards it remained one of the most powerful in the world.

As the years went by, the wounds inflicted by the Civil War slowly healed. Nevertheless, as late as 1683, a group of Cromwell's old supporters attempted to assassinate Charles II on his way back from the races at Newmarket. Many Englishmen continued to remember the days of "Old Noll" with affection.

Time was even kinder to Charles I. The memory of Charles the Martyr was honoured. His noble words at his execution were still remembered: "I go from a corruptible to an incorruptible crown, where no disturbance can be." And both Charles and Cromwell played their part in the development of modern parliamentary government.

Opposite A contemporary woodcut showing the execution of the regicides (1660), as the Royalists exacted their revenge for the death of Charles I.

Table of dates

1625   Charles I becomes King (27th March)

1628   Parliament draws up The Petition of Right, which says that no man should pay a tax that hasn't been approved by parliament.

1629   Charles dissolves parliament, and doesn't call another for eleven years.

1630   Peace concluded with France and Spain.

1634   Ship Money is levied for the first time.

1637   The judges only support the King by seven votes to five in the Ship Money case. More and more people refuse to pay Ship Money. Prayer Book riots in Scotland (July).

1639   The Scots defeat the King in the First Bishops' War.

1640   The Short Parliament (13th April–5th May). Charles dissolves parliament when it refuses to vote him the subsidies he needs.
The Second Bishops' War – the Scots defeat Charles at Newburn and occupy northern England.
The Long Parliament is summoned (3rd November).

1642   Charles attempts to arrest the five members (4th January).
The Royal Standard is raised at Nottingham (22nd August).
The battle of Edgehill (23rd October).
The Eastern Association is formed (10th December).

1643   The battle of Grantham (13th May) – Cromwell defeats the Cavaliers.
The battle of Roundway Down (13th June) – the Cavaliers defeat the Roundheads.
Prince Rupert captures Bristol (26th July).
Cavaliers besiege Gloucester (10th August–5th September).
First battle of Newbury (20th September) is indecisive.
The Scots sign the Solemn League and Covenant, by which they agree to support parliament (25th September).
Defeat of Cavaliers at Winceby (11th October).

1644   The Scots cross into England (16th January).
Battle of Marston Moor (2nd July) – defeat of Prince Rupert.
Second battle of Newbury is again indecisive.

1645   Formation of the New Model Army.
Battle of Naseby (14th June) – defeat of the Cavaliers.
Roundheads capture Bristol (10th September).

1646   Last battle of the war, and defeat of the Cavaliers, at Stow-in-the-Wold (21st March).

Charles surrenders to the Scots (5th May).

1647   The Scots hand Charles over to parliament (28th January).

The King escapes to the Isle of Wight (11th November).

Charles signs a treaty with the Scots, the Engagement (26th December).

1648   The Second Civil War. Cromwell captures Pembroke (11th July).

Scots are defeated by Cromwell at Preston (17th August).

The House of Commons is purged by Colonel Pride, and only a Rump of 45–50 members remains (6th December).

1649   Trial of Charles I (20th–27th January).

Execution of the King (30th January).

Cromwell goes to Ireland. Massacres at Drogheda (11th September) and Wexford (11th October).

1650   Charles II is proclaimed King in Scotland (1st May).

Cromwell defeats the Scots at Dunbar (3rd September).

1651   Charles II is crowned King at Scone (1st January).

The Scots march south, and are defeated at Worcester (3rd September).

Charles escapes to France.

1653   Cromwell expels the Rump Parliament (20th April).

Cromwell becomes Protector (16th December).

1657   Cromwell is given the right to name his successor – the Humble Petition and Advice (25th May).

1658   Battle of the Dunes (4th June). The English help the French to defeat the Spanish.

Death of Oliver Cromwell (3rd September). He is succeeded by his son Richard.

1659   Quarrel between the army and parliament. Richard resigns (25th May).

Lambert expels the Rump Parliament (13th October).

1660   General Monk arrives in London (3rd February).

Parliament agrees to hold new elections (16th March).

Charles II issues the Declaration of Breda (4th April), promising to follow the wishes of parliament.

Charles is invited by parliament to return as King (1st May).

Charles reaches London on his thirtieth birthday (29th May).

Glossary

ARSENAL Place where guns are manufactured, or where they are stored.

BIVOUAC To make camp.

BLOCKADE To prevent anyone from entering or leaving a port, in the hope of starving it into submission.

BRIG A square-rigged sailing ship with two masts.

CARBINE A short musket, originally called a "dragon."

CAVALIER Horseman. Gentleman. The term was applied generally to Royalist supporters in the Civil War.

CLUBMEN Groups of disgruntled countrymen who joined together to attack soldiers during the Civil War.

COMMONWEALTH Term used to describe the period in English history between the execution of Charles I (1649), and the restoration of his son as Charles II (1660).

DEMOBILIZE To pay off soldiers at the end of a war.

DRAGOON A mounted infantryman armed with a carbine.

ENFILADE Gunfire which sweeps a line of troops from end to end.

FLINTLOCK A type of musket, where the gunpowder was ignited by the striking of a flint.

HIGH COMMISSION A royal court which dealt with all matters concerning the church.

IMPEACH To accuse of high treason.

IRONSIDES The troopers recruited by Cromwell.

MATCHLOCK A type of musket in which a lighted cord or "match" carried the flame to the gunpowder.

MILITIA A military force made up of ordinary citizens rather than professional soldiers.

MORTAR A short cannon which fired high into the air instead of parallel to the ground.

ORDINANCE A law passed by parliament without the King's consent.

ORDNANCE The department of the army responsible for weapons and ammunition.

PARLEY To negotiate with the enemy.

PAROLE A prisoner's promise that he will not attempt to escape.

PRIZE A ship captured at sea.

REFORMATION A sixteenth-century movement for the reform of the Catholic church, which led to the establishment of various Protestant churches.

REGICIDES The members of the High Court of Justice who signed Charles I's death warrant. The word "regicide" means killer of the King.

REPUBLIC Term used to describe the period 1649–53, and 1659–60, when England was ruled by parliament alone.

ROYALISTS Supporters of the King.

SHIP MONEY A tax levied on seaports in order to raise money to build ships for the navy.

SPEAKER The officer presiding over the House of Commons.

STAR CHAMBER A special court dealing with offences against the interests of the Crown. It was often very unfair in its decisions, and was abolished in 1640.

TONNAGE AND POUNDAGE Customs duties levied on wine and wool, which were traditionally payable to the King.

TREASON A crime against the King, or against the interests of the State.

TROOPER A soldier with a horse, a cavalryman.

Further Reading

The following books offer a good general introduction to the period:

M. Ashley, *England in the Seventeenth Century* (Penguin, 1952);

S. R. Brett, *The Stuart Century* (Harrap, 1961);

Roger Hart, *English Life in the Seventeenth Century* (Wayland, 1970).

For the younger reader, there are:

J. Lindsay, *Civil War in England* (Muller, 1954);

E. Murphy, *Cavaliers and Roundheads* (Longmans, 1965);

S. Ross, *The English Civil War* (Faber, 1962);

H. R. Williamson, *The Day They Killed the King* (Muller, 1957).

There are also a number of really good historical novels on the period:

G. Heyer, *Royal Escape* (Pan, 1970);

M. Irwin, *The Proud Servant* (Pan, 1971);

M. Irwin, *Stranger Prince* (Pan, 1971);

S. Ross, *Vagabond Treasure* (Hodder & Stoughton, 1956);

R. Sutcliff, *Simon* (Oxford University Press, 1959).

If you want to know more about the leading characters in this book, read:

S. R. Brett, *Oliver Cromwell* (A. & C. Black, 1958);

A. Bryant, *Charles II* (Collins, 1960);

B. Fergusson, *Rupert of the Rhine* (Collins, 1952);

B. Martin, *Our Chief of Men* (Longman's 1960);

C. V. Wedgewood, *Oliver Cromwell* (Duckworth, 1962).

Finally, you can find out more about the fighting from:

C. H. Firth, *Cromwell's Army* (Methuen, 1962).

Index

Picture Credits

The Publishers wish to thank the following for their kind permission to reproduce copyright illustrations on the pages mentioned: the Royal Academy of Arts, *jacket* (front and flaps); the Radio Times Hulton Picture Library, *frontispiece,* 12–13 (top and bottom), 16, 23 (top), 24–25 (top), 26, 40, 44, 46, 47, 50, 56, 60–61, 63, 64, 66, 69, 77, 78, 80, 83 (top and bottom), 84, 87; the Mary Evans Picture Library, 11, 15, 19, 33, 39, 48–49, 59, 70 (left), 75; the Mansell Collection, *jacket* (back), 30, 36–37, 55, 86, 89; the Trustees of the National Portrait Gallery, 34, 84–85. All other pictures appearing in this book are the property of the Wayland Picture Library.
The maps and drawings were done by John Walter.

. Write your name in the
space below